The Good Old Days — They Were Terrible!

The Good Old Days— They Were Terrible!

Otto L. Bettmann

Random House
New York

Library of Congress Cataloging in Publication Data

Bettmann, Otto.
  The good old days—they were terrible!
  1. United States—Civilization—1865–1918—Pictorial works. I. Title.
E169.1.B493 1974   917.3'03'80222   74–6050
ISBN 0-394-48689-7 (hardbound)
ISBN 0-394-70941-1 (paperbound)

Manufactured in the United States of America
98765432

To Anne

Contents

4 Rural Life

The Kitchen—a Vale of Toil:
Farm women: draft horses of
endurance . . .   Fresh Well
Water? The old wooden bucket
delusion . . .   Summer: Buzzing
bugs never ceased to bleed man
and beast . . .   Winter: Smoking
stoves or no heat at all . . .
Bums: How safe was the
countryside? . . .   Farm Children: They lead a life of mind-
dulling blandness . . .   Hard
Times: Mortgages—the worst of
all weeds . . .   Mother Nature:
A wily mistress always ready to
harass the frontiersman . . .
Loneliness: The West was
haunted by loneliness and its
twin sister, despair . . .   The
Lure of the City: "Give me your
rooftops and gas stoves and keep
your acres of prairie"

5 Work

Working Conditions: "The laboring man in this bounteous and
hospitable country has no
ground for complaint" . . .
Accidents: "If you accept a job,
you must accept the risk" . . .
Sweatshops: "A slavery as real
as ever disgraced the South."—
Jacob Riis . . .   Child Labor:
"We take them as soon as they
can stand up" . . .   Standard of
Living: "Steady work? Nothing
steady but want and misery" . . .
Strikes: "We struck because we
were without hope" . . .   Technology: "The demon which is
destroying the people"

6 Crime

Street Crime: "We have to rid
ourselves of this incubus of
evil" . . .   Juvenile Delinquents:
"They have no occupation and
learn no art but to steal" . . .
Police: "Our last prop is the
cop" . . .   New York's Own
Swingers . . .   Graft: "Police
colluding with scoundrels,
coddling villains they are set to
watch" . . .   Prostitution:
"Anybody who denies that
licentiousness in this town is

municipally protected is either a knave or an idiot." . . . Spoilsmen and Plunderers: . . . The Law: "No one respects the law, no one respects the courts, the courts don't respect themselves" . . . The Crime of Punishment. . . Lynching: "What are the atrocities of the Inquisition compared to those of the lynching mobs among us?"

Beware . . . Milk: "A water shortage would put the milkman out of business" . . . Butter: "An unpardonable enormity" . . . Adulteration: "The cupidity of the food manufacturer is not a petty swindle, it is a crime" . . . Children's Food . . . Eating Habits: "Americans don't eat— they gobble, gulp, go" . . . The Western Diet: Hog and hominy —the diet of proverbial ignominy . . . Drinking: "Dramshops yawn at every step" . . . Bibulous Back Country . . . The Saloon: "An institute of vice"

Urban Epidemics: Yellow fever rips the South . . . Disinfection and Quarantine: Half-measures to stem the epidemic tide . . . Frontier Health: "Malarial fever caused more anguish than the threat of scalping Indians" . . . Doctors: A sickly profession . . . Overdrugging: "The standard reproach to medical practice" . . . Surgery: Surgeons performed with the éclat of battle heroes . . . Hospitals: "The one nurse slept in the bathroom—the tub was filled with filthy rubbish" . . . The Mentally Ill: Maltreated and caged like wild beasts . . . Drug Addiction: An apocalypse of horror

Country teacher: A man who had failed at everything bought himself a birch rod and became

a teacher . . . Corporal Punishment: "Lickin' and larnin' goes together, No lickin', no larnin'" . . . Discipline? Pandemonium in the classroom . . . Negro Education: Compulsory Ignorance . . . Dismal Classrooms: "In New York children are forced to attend schools which in foulness could put to shame a refuse vault" . . . Teaching Methods: ". . . each child is treated as if he possessed no individuality, no soul" . . . Teachers: ". . . subsist on a pittance; they must pinch and save until life is not worth living."

Steerage: A traumatic trip led to the Promised Land . . . The Emigrant Train: A Noah's Ark on wheels . . . Ordeals of Railroading: Crowded stations— baggage smashers—demonic stoves . . . Pullman Cars: Infernal dormitories . . . Railroad Food: Scrambling and trampling for the indigestible . . . Commuters: "Most long-suffering and patient of men" . . . Fire on the Water

Gambling: America's oldest diversion deteriorated into a vice . . . Hunting: A rampage of senseless killing . . . Spectator Sports: Big business—fraud— brutality . . . Football: Slugging competitions, gladiatorial shows . . . Pastimes of the Young: "Their opportunities for mischief are greater than those for harmless amusement" . . . Fun with a gun . . . City Parks: Designed for repose and spiritual renewal, they were not immune to urban ills . . . Seaside Leisure: Our beaches are defiled by accumulated junk.

Introduction

THE GOOD OLD DAYS—were they really good? On the surface they appear to be so—especially the period to which this term is most often applied, the years from the end of the Civil War to the early 1900's. This period of history has receded into a benevolent haze, leaving us with the image of an ebullient, carefree America, the fun and charm of the Gilded Age, the Gay Nineties.

But this gaiety was only a brittle veneer that covered widespread turmoil and suffering. The good old days were good for but the privileged few. For the farmer, the laborer,

the average breadwinner, life was an unremitting hardship. This segment of the populace was exploited or lived in the shadow of total neglect. And youth had no voice. These are the people, the mass of Americans, whose adversities this book attempts to chronicle.

Such an endeavor may come as a surprise to those who are familiar with my work. The files of the Bettmann Archive bulge with graphics of what we call the golden past. Many do, indeed, exude an aura of charm and well-being. But there are so many others, less in demand, which give us a totally different picture.

I have always felt that our times have over-rated and unduly overplayed the fun aspects of the past. What we have forgotten are the hunger of the unemployed, crime, corruption, the despair of the aged, the insane and the crippled. The world now gone was in no way spared the problems we consider horrendously our own, such as pollution, addiction, urban plight or educational turmoil. In

most of our nostalgia books, such crises are ignored, and the period's dirty business is swept under the carpet of oblivion. What emerges is a glowing picture of the past, of blue-skied meadows where children play and millionaires sip tea.

If we compare this purported Arcadia with our own days we cannot but feel a jarring discontent, a sense of despair that fate has dropped us into the worst of all possible worlds. And the future, once the resort of hopeful dreams, is envisioned as an abyss filled with apocalyptic nightmares.

My post at "the picture window of history" has given me a more optimistic if less fashionable vista. I have concluded that we have to revise the idealized picture of the past and turn the spotlight on its grimmer aspects. This more realistic approach will show us Gay Nineties man (man in the street, not in the boardroom), as one to be pitied rather than envied. He could but dream of the Utopian miracles that have become part of our everyday life. Compared with him we are lucky—even if dire premonitions darken our days and we find much to bemoan in our society.

Proceeding from such convictions, this may be called a missionary book, a modest personal attempt to redeem our times from

the aspersions cast upon them by nostalgic comparisons. It is a supplemental, revisionary view I offer, necessarily sketchy because of the boundlessness of the subject and the tyranny of book pages that refuse to stretch.

Even if we cast but a cursory glance at the not so good old days and bring them into alignment with our own, we will find much to be grateful for. We are going forward, if but slowly. This fact should move us to view the future in less cataclysmic terms—the future that will see man, in Faulkner's words, "not only endure but prevail."

Traveling on the Hudson River Railroad

1 Air

WHEN THE CIVIL WAR ENDED, the American North was fully mobilized for industry, and forests of smokestacks had grown along with its swelling cities. This was a period of confidence as the country set out boldly to shape a new destiny.

The smoke that billowed over the landscape was seen as a good omen; it meant prosperity. In the industrial communities it was considered a sign of feminine delicacy to complain about the bad air or to have a coughing spell. Mary Gilson, growing up in Pittsburgh in the 1890's, was reprimanded by her parents for complaining about the foul air: "We should be grateful for God's goodness in making work, which made smoke, which made prosperity."

The intense pollution was thus rationalized by its victims and many doctors had only a hazy notion of its effects. Some went so far as to declare that smoke with carbon, sulfur and iodine in it acted as a curative for "lung and cutaneous diseases" and that it killed malaria.

There were other forms of pollution that made life in certain parts of the city unhealthy and degrading: streets caked with animal wastes and the oozings of clogged sewers, and littered with the overflow of uncollected garbage that was piled on the sidewalks. The emanating stenches combined to make New York, in the words of one visitor, a "nasal disaster."

1

Four-Legged Polluters

When pigs roamed Broadway

The ubiquitous pig was suggested as a national emblem.

Broadway's affinity with ham has an enduring quality. In the 1860's, however, two species competed for attention in the heart of the city—one panting on stage, the other squealing and grunting in the streets.

The pig in the city was a paradox—an element of rural culture transposed to urban life. Pigs roamed the streets rooting for food, the stink from their wastes poisoning the air.

Because they ate garbage, the pigs were tolerated to a degree in the absence of adequate sanitation facilities. But this dubious contribution to municipal services was tiny in comparison with the nuisance they caused. From the nation's capital to Midwestern "porkopolis," we are told, squares and parks amounted to public hogpens.

Urbana, Ill., boasted more hogs in the city than people. The human dwellings of Cincinnati in the 1860's comingled with fifty slaughterhouses, which drew a yearly mess of almost half a million pigs through the streets. And in Kansas City the confusion and stench of patrolling hogs were so penetrating that Oscar Wilde observed, "They made granite eyes weep."

Cincinnati: 450,000 porkers passed through the city each year. The transient pig population of Kansas created so much dirt and stench it "made granite eyes shed tears."

New York: Broadway and Fourth Street, 1858, when "his porkship" ruled the town.

Equine smells

In city streets clogged with automobiles, the vision of a horse and buggy produces strong nostalgia. A century ago it produced a different feeling—distress, owing to the horse for what he dropped and to the buggy for spreading it.

Of the three million horses in American cities at the beginning of the twentieth century, New York had some 150,000, the healthier ones each producing between twenty and twenty-five pounds of manure a day. These dumplings were numerous on every street, attracting swarms of flies and radiating a powerful stench. The ambiance was further debased by the presence on almost every block of stables filled with urine-saturated hay.

During dry spells the pounding traffic refined the manure to dust, which blew "from the pavement as a sharp, piercing powder, to cover our clothes, ruin our furniture and blow up into our nostrils."

The 15,000 horses of Rochester, N.Y., produced enough manure in 1900 to cover an acre of ground with a layer 175 feet high. This steadily increasing production caused the more pessimistic observers to fear that American cities would disappear like Pompeii—but not under ashes. The timely arrival of the horseless carriage prevented this, of course. It was widely hoped that the age of polluted air was coming to a close, that cities at long last would be healthier, cleaner, quieter places to live in. But as Proudhon once observed, "human history has a great propensity for surprises."

Sanitation man does battle with manure, Longacre Square, New York, 1900.

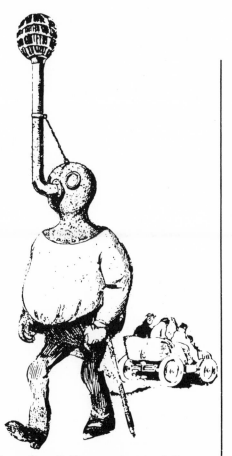

Hopes for relief from equine population were fulfilled, but a more poisonous fume came wafting through the air. (1905)

3

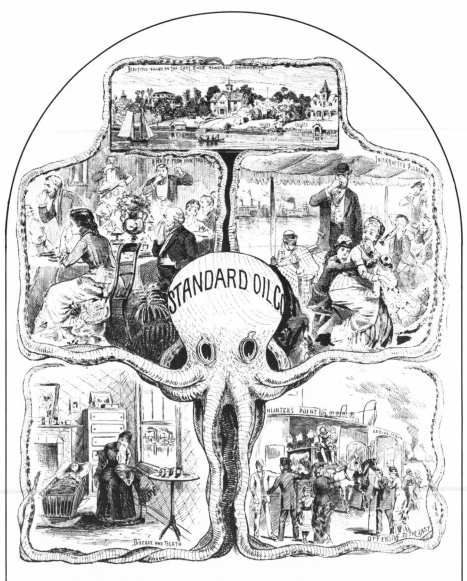

"The Horrible Monster whose tentacles spread disease and death."
Fumes from Standard Oil refineries made New York a "nasal disaster."

Industrial Vapors

They ensnare New York City— Hunter's Point a smelly scandal

"Smog" is a portmanteau word ("smoke" plus "fog") that a Glasgow sanitary engineer coined in 1905. Its widespread use today makes it seem new, but the phenomenon it describes has long existed. Smoke and acrid vapors smothered the industrial cities of the post-Civil War U.S., and municipal control of offending plants was as sparse as clean air in Lower Manhattan.

As the largest city, with 287 foundries and machine shops, a printing industry powered by 125 steam engines, bone mills, refineries and tanneries, New York in 1880 was at one time both major sinner and major victim, symbolizing the unpleasant aspects of industrialization that her sister cities also endured.

The crux of New York's filthy air was Hunter's Point, on the

Thomas Nast cartoon (1881) warned against air pollution by factories at Hunter's Point.

rim of the Bronx, where established industries had moved in force by the late 1870's. Out of sight perhaps, but not out of smell. Grievous odors from the Point poured over Manhattan, affecting all who lived there regardless of rank or address. Frederick Law Olmsted, architect of Central Park, complained that "the stench [was] borne to his residence in

How Hunter's Point's foul odors aggravate the miseries of the sick room.

46th Street, between 7th and 8th Avenues."

But by 1881 even the doggedly patient New Yorkers had coughed enough and angrily compelled the State Board of Health to investigate the origin of their misery. During the inquiry ninety witnesses specified the ingredients that gave the city air its rich flavor: sulfur, ammonia gases, offal rendering, bone boiling, manure heaps, putrid animal wastes, fish scrap, kerosene, acid fumes, phosphate fertilizer and sludge. Such an impressive menu enforced the Board's conclusion that the pollution was harming the citizens' health.

In their testimony, a number of doctors spoke of the violence of the stenches; of oil refineries endlessly puffing black smoke ". . . to produce sickness and depression"; of acid fumes "irritating lungs and throat"; of odors causing "an inclination to vomit."

New Yorkers didn't call it smog in the good old days, and perhaps they were wise. Considering what they breathed daily, the word sounds almost inoffensive.

Arcadian suburbs?

To flee the city for the suburbs in the Gilded Age was often a case of leaving the frying pan for the fire. The miasma from ungraded swampy lands where family refuse decomposed in the sun made living conditions dismal. Municipal services were nonexistent, and the dingy dirty tentacles of Hunter's Point stretched to the furthermost shack.

In Glen Cove, L.I., according to the Board of Health records, the atmosphere was so polluted at times as to produce nausea and make normal breathing difficult. In fear for their health, summer residents petitioned the governor for redress.

The suburbs of
the greatest city
polluted by
garbage-filled marshes.

Garbage Revisited

Some streets smell like bad eggs dissolved in ammonia.

In terms of refuse the human is the richest animal, a fact that is hardly concealed even today by an efficient sanitation system. It was most clearly evident, however, in American cities of the 1860's through the 1880's, where man was surrounded by his own litter much as a champion is surrounded by his trophies. What garbage pickup did exist was capricious and inept.

Again we turn to New York as our "model" city to describe the Golden Age of rubbish. The wastes of daily life, including kitchen slops, cinders, coal dust, horse manure, broken cobblestones and dumped merchandise, were piled high on the sidewalks. There was hardly a block in downtown Manhattan that a pedestrian could negotiate without climbing over a heap of trash or, in rain, wading through a bed of slime.

This endemic mess dramatized how poorly equipped the authorities were to cope with the problems that developing cities encountered after the Civil War. The tumbling disorder caused by overcrowding, the cross purposes of commercial and domestic needs, and the lack of regulation

Garbage dumped on sidewalks impeded pedestrian on downtown streets.

Barrels with cinders from parlor and kitchen stoves send up dust clouds causing teary eyes.

overwhelmed the meager facilities that were available. If liberty had an antic face, it leered from the sidewalks of New York.

Inflation compounded the difficulty of cleanup. In the Northern cities, contractors reneged on their agreements as the currency, like the air, sank in value. Conditions were even worse in Southern towns, such as Memphis and New Orleans, where sewerage facilities were more primitive and municipal supervision criminally lax.

New York's sidewalks were lined with unharnessed trucks, beneath and between which dirtier citizens threw their filth. A foreign visitor said of this antique parking problem that it made the city look "like a huge dirty stable." The wagons were coveted as a refuge by lovers and criminals, and one truck was distinguished by providing overnight shelter for a newly arrived Joseph Pulitzer. An 1895 ordinance to prohibit

this parking nuisance was impeded by truckmen who removed a wheel from their vehicles to prevent the city from towing them away. We can only speculate what such spirited fellows might have done to a parking meter.

New York Harbor Everglades: rivers clogged with dead horses, discarded vehicles, machines.

8

Traffic impeded by garbage thrown between unharnessed trucks.

THE MUSEUM OF THE CITY OF NEW YORK

NEW YORK DEPARTMENT OF SANITATION

Wind

"Wherever the wind blows, the foul corruption is carried."

In nature's scheme of things the wind is messenger; it will carry with perfect fidelity to natural laws the scent of lilac or volcanic ash. And what man writes in the wind will be delivered back to him with immutable certainty. During the headlong celebration of industrial power that marked the Gilded Age, man wrote in it with septic muck, and the wind carried it straight back to him— to his nostrils and eyes and lungs.

In the opinion of *Leslie's Weekly* (1881), "... no dumping-ground, no sewer, no vault contains more filth or in greater variety than [does] the air in certain parts of [New York] city during the long season of drought.... No barrier can shut it out, no social distinction can save us from it; no domestic cleanliness, no private sanitary measures can substitute a pure atmosphere for a foul one."

"When the dust is upon the city, it becomes a terrible place to dwell in. Its sharp lung-piercing powder makes us the greatest sufferers from catarrh and consumption." Scene on Franklin Street, New York, 1881.

FRANKLIN ST. AND W. BROADW

Summary

"The great foul city emanating poison at every pore"

As warm-blooded creatures, we have always had more success coping with cold than with heat. The air conditioner, blessing that it is, alters but does not reverse that fact. Nonetheless, in hot weather we are cooler today by several degrees—without artificial help—than the city dwellers of the past.

The record shows that the "good old summer days" were often unbearable, indoors and out. New York City, for instance, was hotter then, with lower buildings that offered little protection from the sun. And the clothing of the period—heavy suits, long underwear, starched shirts plus vests, girdles and voluminous petticoats—added a penitential excess to the citizens' misery. Delirium and sunstroke were commonplace; a heat wave in August 1896 caused the deaths of some three thousand humans and two thousand horses.

The windowless room was another feature of city life that exacerbated summer hardships. An 1894 survey found 6576 New York slum families living in such "inside" rooms, where during a heat wave stagnant air hung for weeks at equatorial temperatures. Air shafts provided by

Humane help for horses.

Horse-cure for humans.

landlords to circumvent an 1879 ban on these rooms were used as garbage chutes, infecting the oven-hot air with a rancid smell.

In the slums, conditions were most pitiable. Seeking refuge outdoors from their furnacelike quarters, the poor lay in the alley-ways and streets, where, according to a witness, the pavement was turned into "masses of fire in which the air quivers and palpitates." The nights brought no relief, only a still, sleepless languor filled with apprehension for the morrow.

New York's slum dwellers escape from their windowless hovels. "On a hot night the streets are filled with families all panting and praying for fresh air."

Chicago

"Having seen it . . . I desire urgently never to see it again. Its air is dirt."

Rudyard Kipling made these remarks about Chicago, a city that during the Gilded Age yielded nothing to New York in the breadth and virulence of its pollution. Which city was dirtier was an academic question, but one visitor noted a difference in the character of Chicago's industry-created climate: "The smoke . . . has a peculiar aggressive individuality . . ."

It is possible that the observer was a romantic, attributing to Chicago's pollution the pugnacious, emotional qualities that the city was noted for. However, its very location on low prairie flats militated against the chance of becoming a healthy place to live in. In early Chicago, natural drainage was nonexistent, flooding habitual, and the Chicago River fetid "with grease so thick on its surface it seemed a liquid rainbow."

The city tackled these problems with the buoyant spirit of the frontier, literally raising itself — on pilings and vast land-fill — seven to twelve feet above the prairie. Its population — only five thousand souls in 1840 — grew to a startling one million by 1890. The great fire of 1871 did not stop Chicago's blustering advance; indeed the fire and smoke it produced may have had a baptismal effect on its people, tempering them for the ordeal to come.

As it grew during the 1870's into a major transportation center,

Swampy Chicago, built at prairie level, was crisscrossed by fetid inlets. The river floated grease "so thick it seemed a liquid rainbow."

with eight railroads, a busy port, and heavy industry keeping apace, Chicago's pollution assumed a permanent, almost solid quality. "During my stay of one week, I did not see in Chicago anything but darkness, smoke, clouds of dirt," reported the Italian dramatist Giuseppe Giacosa. "One morning, when I happened to be on a high railroad viaduct, the city seemed to smolder, a vast, unyielding conflagration."

The largest assemblage of stockyards in the world added a pungent flavor to Chicago's air. The stockyards were the city's pride, and visitors were constantly being dragged to see them. After witnessing the disemboweling ceremonies, Lord Coleridge pleaded to be led outside or he "never could eat sausage again."

A feature of the city's outlying districts, which lacked paved streets, was the sandstorms blown by the wind from Lake Michigan, stinging the eyes and making travel a hardship. A visitor remarked: "How a person can navigate this dirty city at night is a mystery to me."

Because of its assault on eye, ear, nose and throat in the good old days, Chicago was rarely mentioned without the adornment of various uncomplimentary adjectives. Today it is known affectionately as the Windy City. And that is a monumental achievement.

Smells from garbage heaps aggravated by exudation from stockyard poisoned Chicago air. Children shown are searching for food.

Pittsburgh

"Nothing dingier and more dispiriting can be imagined."

At the turn of the century Pittsburgh and its environs along the Monongahela Valley boasted some 14,000 chimneys (most of them belonging to iron and steel plants) that provided à 24-hour barrage of soot, ashes and glowing embers. A Hungarian visitor, Count Vay de Vaya, described it as "a noisome vomit, killing everything that grows—trees, grass and flowers." Workers were hardly able to breathe in this atmosphere "worthy of Satan himself."

Thousands, moreover, were compelled to live close to these factories—in drab, unpainted shanties with smoke belching right through the windows, the backyards thick with mud and strewn with beer kegs and rubbish. No attempt was made to separate industry and human habitation. On the contrary, companies welcomed such proximity because it enabled them to exert tighter control over the workers.

Merely keeping clean became a problem in Pittsburgh—even for the middle class that lived apart from the industrial sections. Around 1900 the residents spent $1,500,000 on extra laundry work and $750,000 a year for extra general cleaning, according to Chamber of Commerce figures. Cincinnati had similar problems. People's hands and faces were constantly grimy, clean collars quickly acquired a thin layer of soot, and the bituminous coal dust gave clothes hung out in the weekly wash a permanent yellow tinge.

But Pittsburghers were not to be daunted. They pronounced the city "one of the healthiest in the United States. . . . People work so hard here they don't notice the smoke."

Farther West

Contrary to the sanitized view that Hollywood gives us, Western

Bridge Street, Helena, Montana. Lacking municipal facilities, frontier towns reeked of filth.
Hitching places for horses turned into cesspools.

towns were actually quite dirty, and so were the cowpokes who frequented them. The horses— everybody had at least one— created steamy cesspools around the hitching posts, where flies plagued man and beast and a vile odor abounded. Frequently oxen and cattle contributed to the mess, and after a rainfall the streets were filled with a yellow-brown ooze.

Leadville, Colo., reported a morass on its Main Street 18 inches deep in which the wooden sidewalks formed a "sort of raft," an ideal nest for rats. This mess seeped into pools to be pumped up as drinking water so putrid "it made liquor drinking a virtue."

Pioneers trekked westward to breathe what they expected would be the fresh air of small frontier towns. What they often encountered was air like that of a malarial swamp.

Pittsburgh in the 1890's: "The realm of Vulcan couldn't be more filthy with burning fires spurting flames on every side."

Traffic jam, Broadway, New York, 1869. "A serried mass of seething humanity." A lady in her landau might find herself close to a brewery stallion as his steaming urine cascaded to the pavement.

2 Traffic

TRAFFIC AND HORSEPOWER are indivisible. Today horsepower fills the streets in mechanical disguise. In 1870 horsepower filled the streets with heavy, sweating substance.

The horse and cart, in one shape or another, spans much of history to the twentieth century as the principal means of land travel and the principal cause of traffic jams. Both Julius Caesar and Grover Cleveland traveled by horse and cart, and almost two thousand years after Caesar's imperial edict banned chariots (except those of the vestal virgins) from Rome's clogged streets the cities of the New World groaned under the press of wagon, beast and man.

Indeed a study of the period suggests that the traffic jam, as a monster spawned by civilization, reached hideous proportions before the turn of the century. A traffic report from Lower Broadway in 1872: "What a jam! Stages, carriages, cartmen, expressmen, pedestrians all melted together in one agglomerate mess!"

All "seemed to be driven by some frantic demon of haste." Even the American cat, was supercharged "as though late for an appointment." To call a present-day traffic jam chaotic is not entirely accurate; it has too dormant, too regimented a quality about it. Chaos was the stuff of jams in the good old days, and there were no angry Caesars to cry "Halt!"

Streetcars:
a paradise for pickpockets
and the domain of
insolent conductors.

Horsecar

Inferno on wheels

The horse-drawn streetcar was a passenger's inferno and a pickpocket's paradise. A precaution suggested by one traveler: "Before boarding a car, prudent persons leave their purses and watches in the safe deposit company and carry bowie knives and derringers."

In winter the streetcar became a rolling icebox, the stove on board more a symbol than a threat to the frigid temperatures. Like the horses up front, the stove was chronically underfed.

In summer the atmosphere was even more disagreeable. Fumes from unwashed bodies and beery breath thickened the ambient stench of tobacco juice to a porridge of nausea.

If the streetcar horses were notoriously maltreated, so too were the passengers. Although not flogged, they were commonly regarded as indistinguishable from freight.

"Move forward, please."

More than half of those who ride are obliged to stand.
"Toes are trod on; Hats are smashed;
Dresses soiled, Hoopskirts crashed."

Drivers received $12
a week for a 16-hour day.
Their demand for a 12-hour day
was branded as "communistic"
by State Assemblyman
Teddy Roosevelt.

At rush hour—a self-contradicting term since the crush of traffic precludes speed—conductors loaded as many as eighty passengers into a car designed for twenty-five. The buildup of pressure inside the car forced much of this human baggage through window and door openings to cling to the sides like squid to a rock.

However crowded the car, there was always "room for one more." Streetcar owners encouraged their conductors to "pack them in," and took gleeful pride in the heavy "straphanger profits" they tallied up at year end.

"Men and women are
indecently crushed without regard for
that personal dignity we prize."
—*William Dean Howells*

Crossing the Street

"It takes more skill to cross Broadway . . . than to cross the Atlantic in a clamboat."

Policeman helps enraged lady across.

In the hundred years from the 1870's to the 1970's, fear has changed partners on city streets. Today, while the pedestrian still grouses and the elderly admit mild fright, it is the driver who trembles at the thought of hitting a pedestrian. In the 1870's it was the pedestrian who was terrified. With never a halt in the flow of traffic, on Broadway and other thoroughfares the pedestrian faced such hazards in the riptide of commerce that his lot was little better than a deer's in open season.

Strangers were transfixed by the sight of the traffic-choked streets. "How to cross Broadway

Reckless drivers raced along Broadway "defying law, delighting in destruction."

is one of the problems of life in New York," observed *Home and Hearth* in 1874; "even the nimblest of New Yorkers stands on the curbstone and lays out a plan before marching across the thronged thoroughfare."

The engine of city mayhem was the horse. Underfed and nervous, this vital brute was often flogged to exhaustion by pitiless drivers, who exulted in pushing ahead "with utmost fury, defying law and delighting in destruction." Runaways were common. The havoc killed thousands of people. According to the National Safety Council, the horse-associated fatality rate was ten times the car-associated rate of modern times.

Boxes clogging sidewalk. Merchant used street for storage.

Truckman beats coachman who has refused to give way.

"Vast chasm open beneath every turn as new rails are laid" ... Harper's advised, "The next man who tears up Broadway should be lynched."

Early safety poster warns that railroads will take over cities, make Philadelphia a suburb of New York, usurp all streets, maim and kill children.

The absence of a public outcry against this chaos puzzled foreign observers; it did not seem logical that a spirited, pugnacious people could be complacent under such abuse. There was one practice, however, which provoked an uproar of protest. The steam railroads often laid track right through the center of town, thus creating another and more lethal crossing menace.

Railroad designers had a preoccupation with straight lines. Curved track incurred trouble and higher costs, and so new construction was laid through towns rather than around them. The owners saw nothing wrong in this because in fact, and in law, the towns belonged to them. The railroad companies drew the map of the urban age. "Altoona was a child of the Pennsylvania. The Lackawanna turned Slocum's Hole into Scranton."

In the iron horse, the street horse now had a rival in bloodletting, itself frequently the victim. Almost every town was

marked by the X's of grade crossings, which were frequently the scene of fatal accidents. In one year Chicago accounted for a record 330 grade-crossing deaths; Philadelphia was a close second, while New York had "only" 124. At a Chicago crossing sixteen lives were lost in one accident. "No one was punished."

Aesthetically, the situation was equally bad, with locomotives adding their din, smoke and vibrations to the ugliness and tension of urban America. For the pedestrian, this produced what Lewis Mumford has called "immolation under the wheels of the puffing juggernaut."

History tells us how Moses crossed the Sinai Desert with his people and that Caesar crossed the Rubicon with his men. But the pedestrian who successfully crossed the streets of yesterday's urban America is unremembered. There was simply no glory in it, only the certain knowledge that he would have to cross again.

"The railroad tracks run through the busiest streets, killing pedestrians, scaring horses . . . Death on the track is a standing American headline."

Overhead railroad drawn by diminutive steam engines scattered
ashes and cinders on unwary pedestrian below.
Harper & Bros. offices at left.

The El

"New York was made for street-railways — not railways for New York."

There were only two really happy days in the history of New York's famous "El": the day the trains started operation in 1868 and the day their dismantling was completed. Close to a century of confusion lay in between.

How did it all come about?

In the 1870's and 1880's the city meant New York, and New York meant Manhattan Island. Immigrants tumbled in by the thousands, descending as if by gravity to the lower half of the 9-by-2½-mile slab in the estuary of the Hudson River. That was where the boats docked and the trains stopped; that was where the money flowed, where opportunity knocked. But the crowding in lower Manhattan became intolerable. Of a total population of 942,292 in the city, 477,804 were squeezed into the area between 14th Street and City Hall,

The El: "Through it metaphorically iron has entered the city's soul."

City dwellers became insomniacs through noise from rattling trains, which at night hovered above streets "like gigantic fireflies."

according to the census of 1870. Unless an effective transportation system was provided to move people uptown, the city would collapse under the pressure. The elevated railroad became—for better and for much worse—New York's vehicle of "transit reform."

The Gilbert Elevated Railway of 1868 running along Greenwich Street was the first experimental piece of the system that was to become known as the El. Within a decade it was joined by the Third Avenue Railroad between City Hall Park and 42nd Street and in the 1880's many miles of New York's principal avenues were covered by "streets on stilts." Sunlight was stifled, traffic frustrated by the hulking iron pillars, and in the semidarkness pedestrians cringed in fear of falling ashes, oil and cinders.

Ugly, dirty, depressing, the El became a blight on New York City. Aside from the smoke and dust, the rattling, screeching trains made buildings adjacent to the tracks tremble and created "a noise so exasperating that it amounted to positive pain." They became a monumental nuisance, marking, in Mumford's phrase "the end of urban acceptability."

Slow and unreliable, the trains played havoc with traffic they were intended to relieve. During rush hours, as William Dean Howells describes it, "Every seat is taken . . . in the aisle people standing and swaying miserably, crushed together without regard for that personal dignity we prize."

It is not clear whom the elevated railroads displeased most: those who traveled on them, those who walked under them, or those who lived near them. But it is clear who liked them: their owners, who with memorable impudence were moved to declare, "Street railways were not made for New York—New York was made for street railways."

All in all, the effects of the El were not wholly negative. At best, it toughened New Yorkers for the future by teaching them the dangers of giving a public trust to those who could least be trusted.

"Unless the people slaughter the speculators we shall have the sky filled with buzzing locomotives."

Winter

"Snowplows—triumphs of awkwardness"

There is no room for snow in the city, but it falls on it just the same, heaping the streets with chaos and the mayor with crises. In a heat wave the residents look to the gods for relief, but in a snowstorm they turn, quixotically, to his Honor. An untimely snowstorm in New York can cost the mayor his reelection, as the budget melts away and his citizens tramp angrily through glacial streets.

Snow removal is a troublesome, costly operation, but the results today are a singular success when compared with those of the 1870's and 1880's. In fact,

the word "removal" when applied to that period grossly overstates the operation. The snow remained; it was merely shifted, if at all, a few yards.

Keeping the streets clear for the horse trolleys was the uppermost priority, and cumbersome eight-team plows banked the sidewalks with enormous heaps of snow. Often becoming stuck themselves, the plows aggravated the public's misery by blocking the roads to other traffic. Extra horses sometimes were harnessed to free the machines, and an uproar ensued as the straining animals were lashed by their handlers and cursed by onlookers.

It was not uncommon for trolley passengers to disembark and push their car as its horses floundered, unable to find their footing on the icy surface. The less ambitious helped the driver whip his animals. Pedestrians could fall all they wanted to, but if a horse fell it would delay the trolley car, and that could not be tolerated.

Snowplows, "triumphs of awkwardness, pushed snow onto sidewalks, making them impassable for pedestrians."

Electric Trolleys

Slow passage in fast cars

The electric trolley car, introduced to city streets in 1887, was a sophisticated advance in transport technology, welcomed by people who were accustomed to its heretofore cruder and more bellicose apparatus.

It provided the catalyst to urban expansion, and by the turn of the century over one million New Yorkers had resettled in outlying districts. Heralded as fast, cheap transportation, the electric trolley attracted the mass of citizens, who once more were to experience the unhappy discrepancy between promise and delivery.

Impeded continually by traffic snarls they helped create, the trolleys seldom reached their design speed of 20 to 25 miles an hour. For long stretches they were forced to keep "step" behind horsecars, which were not abandoned when their electrified successors appeared.

The mixed marriage of incompatible modes of transport was a bad one, but it persisted for years. Monumental tie-ups occurred daily, and long into the age of electricity the average speed of urban traffic was determinedly prescribed by the horse. Along with the inconvenience electric cars brought to metropolitan centers came the unattractive jumble of overhead wires. Chicago ran her cars in pairs through the busiest streets, an insane concession to laissez faire. H. G. Wells, usually sympathetic toward urban growth, found Chicago streets in 1906 "simply chaotic—one hoarse cry for discipline." (The discipline came later, with municipal ownership of the lines.)

Moreover, the 5-cent fare of the day (10 cents on the El) was not considered cheap, especially by workmen with large families. Streetcar fares cost low-income travelers almost 10 percent of their pay, which averaged less than 25 cents an hour.

Cable cars near "Deadman's Curve," Broadway and 14th Street, gave New Yorkers "a new anxiety and worry."

Trolleys were slowed by
horsedrawn vehicles.
In winter, snapped wires
caused fear of electrocution.

Chicago streets were called "one hoarse cry for discipline" by H. G. Wells in 1906.

SUNSHINE AND SHADOW IN NEW YORK.

New York, "the filthiest, wealthiest town" in the world:
on 23rd Street, the Stewart mansion with its 18-foot ceilings;
downtown, shaky firetraps—bedrooms without windows.

3 Housing

THE RAGS-AND-RICHES paradox of America during the Gilded Age was nowhere more visible than in New York City. The poor lived close by the rich, and the contrast in their housing embarrassed those of sensitivity, troubled those of conscience, and mocked those of faith. Tenements huddled pitifully in the shadow of mansions, and next to the splendors of Fifth Avenue were the rocky wastes of a shantytown that in the 1880's extended from 42nd to 110th Street. This counterpoint of squalor and luxury was compared, by a British traveler, to a lady with diamonds around her neck and her toes sticking out of shabby shoes.

New York's reputation of the period was that of a gay, raffish high society, whose ostentation and carryings-on diverted attention from the despair and the realities of life among the poor and lower-middle class. Decent accommodation at modest rentals was nonexistent, as a "housing famine" proved an economic calamity to the mass of city residents. Trapped in serfdom, poor families were unable to escape the slums, and unwilling too, perhaps, because of ethnic ties and the proximity to casual jobs. "Except for those who are very rich, it is impossible to live in the city with any degree of decency." Even in the fine brownstones life was commonly short of the serene orderliness suggested by their façades.

Townhouses

"Constantly demanding structures with few alleviating graces"

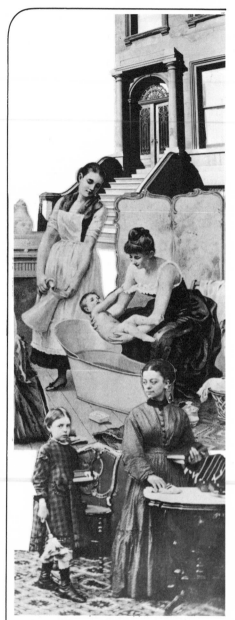

Bathing baby: a splashy ordeal, requiring hot water from the kitchen stove.

Homes overloaded with "super-annuated trash" suffered from street dust, cinders from stoves.

Kerosene replacing whale oil as illuminant proved "explosive as gunpowder." In 1880, 39 percent of all New York fires were caused by defective lamps.

Townhouses give a city architectural balance; they soften the heavy presence of commercial and institutional buildings. Among the fashionable of New York it is now considered chic to own one. The handsome façades have not been altered since the Gilded Age, but the interiors have, and for good reason. In their heyday these houses were stuffy, difficult to maintain and occasionally injurious to health.

A basic problem was the polluted air that permeated almost all sections of the city. Brownstone residents were advised to keep their windows permanently shut against outside air, which was "redolent with a mixture of soot, factory vapors, and animal stenches." Indoors, because of the lack of ventilation, the air was comparable in quality, if not worse. Sewer gas from primitive drainage systems posed a constant peril to health; dampness and odors plagued the homes of rich and poor alike.

The indoor air was befouled further by the standard coal stove, which gobbled oxygen in exchange for soot and dust. Central steam heat provided a costly ($2000–$4000) alternative in the

1880's, but the early radiators were afflicted by a novel form of nuisance, water hammer and hissing. One wonders if the brownstone resident annoyed by these noises was consoled by the thought that the air was cleaner.

In one area of personal care, the Victorians appeared untroubled. They seldom bathed. Glorification of the bathroom is a modern fetish. In 1882 only 2 percent of New York's homes had water connections, and these in all probability were leaky and, if attached to a stove, dangerous. Bathing was considered harmful by some doctors, and one, C. E. Sargent, described it as "a needless waste of time." In an ornate or overstuffed townhouse regular chores, from bathing the baby (generally approved) to dusting and cleaning, were a grinding toil, but most wearisome of all was cooking. Preparation of a Victorian dinner was a monumental task in a kitchen of spartan design.

The servant problem was insoluble. In general, American girls were too proud to seek menial jobs, and immigrant girls were unsatisfactory as a result of the language barrier, their temperament, or their ignorance of domestic social customs. And capable girls refused to stay because of the enormous workload, the townhouse requiring "an unremitting war with its refusal to stay clean, orderly, warm, ventilated, nourishing and pleasant."

With plumbing notoriously shoddy, leakage of sewer gas through cellar joints posed a constant threat to family health.

Servants were hard to get—and harder to keep, since they preferred factory work to "being on tap from 6 a.m. to 11 p.m."

35

Tenant Trouble

*I am the landlord—my rights
none can dispute
I am the lord though they call
me a brute*

In public affection the landlord's rating was comparable to that of the kidnaper; and the richer he was, the more likely he was to deserve it. His victim, the tenant, is today protected by the law, but a hundred years ago he was vulnerable, ignorant and utterly misused.

New York's soaring population —augmented by the continuing influx of Europeans—aggravated the housing shortage and inflated real estate values. Keen as foxes to the scent of weaker game,

speculators piously came to the rescue by building the cheapest form of tenements.

Cracked walls, sagging floors and a total absence of fire exits were features of these neglected buildings, whose dingy overcrowded rooms drew extortionate rents. Landlords bullied poor and middle-class families with yearly rent increases and unpardonably brutal evictions.

Boarding houses

For New Yorkers who became casualties of the rent spiral the boarding house offered a solution, though not an ideal one. For $3 to $5 a week the clerk or working girl could find refuge here, along with childless couples, adventurers and ne'er-do-wells. Together they comprised a true cross section of America's transient population—a culture of the homeless who were bound to a fixed place by neither blood nor tradition.

No invention of the Gilded Age, the boarding house had flourished before the Civil War

A tenant's sketch
of the landlord.

"Camp in a covered wagon"
was the wry advice
to New Yorkers
caught between low incomes
and high rents.

in frontier cities and towns as a vital element in the nation's growth. Charles Dickens, among others, missed their significance when he waspishly compared America's rootless ways with those of the English.

Domestic moralists saw them as a threat to Victorian rectitude that loosened family ties and encouraged sinful liaisons. No doubt these dangers existed, but for legions with meager resources the boarding house was home.

"Boarding houses are unnatural and the result of an overcrowded civilization." The New York of the 1870's was called "one vast boarding house."

No court procedures were needed to dispossess tenants. In 1884, over 43,000 New York families were evicted for failure to pay rent.

Money-bagged landlord stands in front of his "crack tenements," erected with no concern for tenants' comfort, safety or health.

Conglomerate Living

Middle-class apartment houses were crammed . . .

The need for the apartment house existed for many years before its evolution. The boarding house and tenement were too little; the townhouse, too much. The intense frustration of city life literally forced the development of the apartment building, which was to convert millions of Americans into "cliff dwellers."

The flight from private dwellings began with the well-to-do, whose townhouses had become a financial burden. Richard M. Hunt created the prototype of a new style of housing in his Stuyvesant Apartments on 18th Street in New York. Contrary to dire predictions that New Yorkers would never consent to live "on

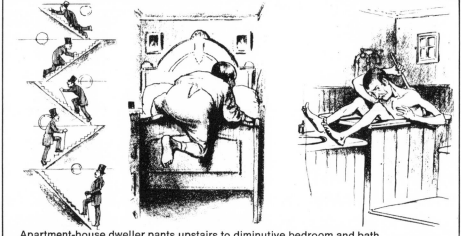

Apartment-house dweller pants upstairs to diminutive bedroom and bath.

mere shelves under a common roof," this building and similar ones that followed it proved very successful. Class privilege was safeguarded by rents up to $3000 for seven rooms.

Reassured by the acceptance of communal living by the wealthy, real estate entrepreneurs built lower-rent apartment houses for the middle class. But these structures, which soon mushroomed in American cities, were little more than glorified tenements; and the style of living that was a pleasure for the rich became, in imitation, a curse to the wage

Higher buildings were made possible by installation of elevators. Passengers feared that cable might snap and send them crashing to death.

earner. As a contemporary observed, "Reasonable apartments are not good, and good apartments are not reasonable."

Families were shelved in layers, sharing floors that were subdivided into several apartments—three or four tiny rooms providing no insulation from the neighbors' cooking smells or babies' squallings. Garbage removal and sanitary facilities were comparably wretched, and overcrowding made the buildings "more difficult to manage than the tenement houses of the slum districts."

... Fires threatened their residents.

As the size and number of apartment buildings increased, so too did the danger that a fire would turn them into blazing prisons. Of course, they were not the only firetraps, but they accounted for the heaviest loss of life in the great conflagrations of the period. Between 1870 and 1906 four American cities—Chicago, Boston, Baltimore and San Francisco—burned to the ground, a record unmatched anywhere else in the world. Boston's assessment of its yearly fire damage—$1 to $1.5 million—was ten times greater than that of a European city of comparable size.

The frequency and destructiveness of fires in American cities were blamed on shoddy construction and the use of flammable materials in the construction of "fireproof" apartments. Even as late as 1904, after steel had replaced the less heat-resistant cast iron for building, 7000 lives were lost in city fires.

Nowhere is the fireman more celebrated than in the United States. And for sound, historical reasons.

Apartment houses for the less affluent were flimsily built, and lacking insulation, became fire traps.

Workers and Squatters

"It is a defamation to use the word 'home' for their pest-ridden shanties."

Invalid Pennsylvania coal miner with children in front of makeshift company shack.

Squatters near Central Park. "When eviction notices were served, squatters fed them to their goats."

A close-knit family, animals and all. Garbage was thrown into the backyard.

The word "shanty" is of Gaelic origin and means old house. To the laborers who lived in shanties in the coal regions of Pennsylvania, the meaning must have seemed unnecessarily flattering.

Strewn over the landscape like so many abandoned, rotting crates —some actually perched, with macabre inspiration, on slag heaps—they were home to thousands of European workers and their families.

The industrialists who provided these homes, which dismayed even the humblest of the wretched newcomers, rationalized easily: "[they] were only foreigners . . . there was no use giving them anything decent, for they weren't used to decent surroundings and wouldn't appreciate them if they had them."

In New York, meanwhile, the same type of dwelling had taken flourishing root on the periphery of the city, which until the turn of the century was largely open land. For thousands of families, squatting in their own wretched box was more endurable than life in a tenement. In the Good Old Days, common alternatives were degrees of ignominy.

The formless squatter encampments surrounded the city like a ring of scum around a tub. Built of discarded boxes and construction-site refuse, the hovels presented a grotesque counterpoint to fashionable areas nearby. When the American Museum of Natural History opened its doors in 1877, it stood in majestic relief amid the wreckage of a new civilization.

The inhabitants of shantytown lived within the city but did not belong to it. Democracy's flotsam, they lived in unspeakable squalor —ignored, resented and, in good times, pitied.

Cross section of a New York tenement house, its inhabitants beset by grinding poverty, filth and disease, "drunk, bestial, vile . . . steadily sinking."
In these dungeons, parents were demoralized and children became depraved.
"Fever has taken a perennial lease and will obey no summons to quit."

The Slums

Uninhabitable pens crowded to suffocation

A hundred years after the Founding Fathers had dedicated themselves to forming a new nation based on man's innate dignity, millions of its citizens wallowed in degradation.

These were the slum dwellers: the losers in the system that exalted the individual. They came by the slums through a quirk of fate, and once in them they fell victim to plagues of body and mind that produced crime, drunkenness, disease and early death in a remorseless cycle.

The authors of the Constitution could not have foreseen this blight on their earnest hopes. The slums, curiously, were a natural result of the optimism that marked the good old days, the rampant growth of industry and population that turned towns into cities and adventurers into exploiters with bewildering speed. As always, the devil had to have his due, and he was paid in slums.

Cleveland's infected area was known as the Flats; in St. Louis it was Cross Keys and Clabber Alley; in Boston, the North End. Chicago's extensive slums adjoined the stockyards, street after street of pitiful wreckage lacking sanitation, drainage, ventilation, light and safety. But worst of all, typically, was New York.

Between 1868 and 1875 an estimated 500,000 lived in New York's slums—about half the city's population. As many as eight persons shared a living room that was 10 by 12 feet and a bedroom 6 by 8 feet. One tenement on the Lower East Side was packed with 101 adults and 91 children.

Among the indignities they were forced to suffer—all noted by city health inspectors—were vile privies; dirt-filled sinks; slop oozing down stairwells; children urinating on the walls; dangerously dilapidated stairs; plumbing pipes pockmarked with holes that emitted sewer gases so virulent they were flammable.

Even among slum residents there was a ghastly hierarchy, at the bottom of which were the cellar dwellers. Their quarters acted as a repository for street filth that washed down on rainy days, caking a floor that men, women and children often shared with goats and pigs. "The inmates exhibited the same lethargic habits as animals burrowing in the ground."

An absorbing footnote is the fact that the rent per square foot of the slums of the period was 25 to 35 percent higher than that of apartments in fashionable uptown New York. The slumlords, unable to resist profits of 50 to 70 percent on their original investment, squeezed tenants mercilessly. Politicians, exclusive club members and even churches were among the owners, who no doubt rationalized their greed as the mine operators did for their workers' shacks.

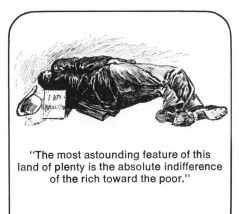

"The most astounding feature of this land of plenty is the absolute indifference of the rich toward the poor."

Slum Children

Their home is the street

In 1874 a New York social worker, Etta Angel Wheeler found a little girl wandering naked through the slums. The child had been beaten and slashed by her drunken foster mother and then chased from home. Unable to find a haven for her, Miss Wheeler asked the Society for the Prevention of Cruelty to Animals for help; it was decided that "the child being an animal" the Society would give it protection.

An animal—the end product of slum life. Disfigured by the bestiality of home, thousands of urchins wandered the streets—an 1880 estimate had 100,000 loose in New York—cunning, predatory, with an instinct for survival that rivaled an alley cat's. They slept under doorways, in discarded boxes and barrels; they fought, blasphemed, begged and stole; and in the end they gravitated to prostitution and crime. It was the natural succession of their unnatural orbit.

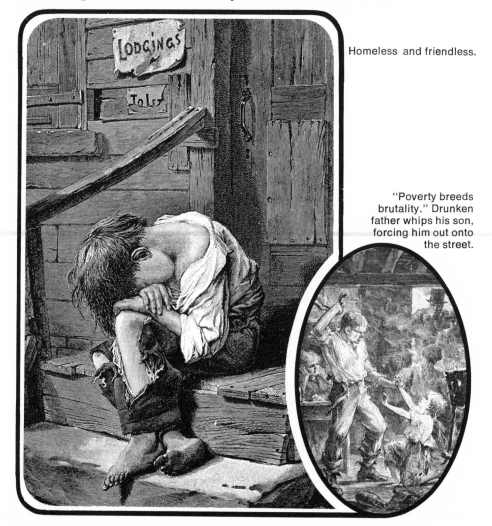

Homeless and friendless.

"Poverty breeds brutality." Drunken father whips his son, forcing him out onto the street.

Boys: lodging houses, overcrowded with applicants, rejected boys with "homes."

Abandoned children slept under stairs, crept into ashcans to escape the cops.

Girl traders hardened by alley-cat existence fell into prostitution.

Atop a steam grating, half-frozen street urchins try to catch some heat.

Throwing slop and leftover food outside the kitchen door poisoned wells.
Yard animals added to the toxic seepage.

4 Rural Life

IT IS DIFFICULT TO THINK OF country life without illusion. We are always tempted to invest it with virtues that appear to have been corrupted in urban culture. And rural folklore, shamelessly exploited, intensifies images of idyllic simplicity and bedrock values. Country living presents visions of nostalgia to soothe city nerves. But these visions are grossly inaccurate especially when applied to the good old days. Country life in the post-Civil War era was an unremitting hardship. The farmer and his family toiled fourteen hours a day merely to sustain themselves, primarily on a landscape that lacked the picturesque inspiration of Currier & Ives' prints.

Nor did their endless drudgery reward the farmers with prosperity; during the economic distress of 1870-1900 few small and middle-sized farms produced anything beyond bare subsistence, and many were foreclosed. In place of a neat rose garden, an expanse of muck and manure surrounded the farmhouse, sucking at boots and exuding a pestilential stench that attracted swarms of flies, ticks and worms to amplify the miseries of man and beast. The elemental task of survival precluded any concern for hygiene or sanitary installations. And the punitive winter brought with it isolation and terrible loneliness.

The Kitchen—
A Vale of Toil

Farm women: draft horses of endurance

A recurring image of late nine-teenth-century farm life is a charming, sun-filled kitchen where an Aunt Polly—to cries of "Lan' sakes!"—empties second helpings of steaming vittles onto plates that reflect calico, freckles and perfect adjustment. With the possible exception of the gentry, history offers a different picture.

The country kitchen, as the heart of the farmhouse and its only heated area, served equally as dining room, living room and washroom. It was primitive and usually crowded beyond the point of intimacy.

Cooking, the kitchen's major activity, was done in an open-hearth fireplace with crooks and arms or, more likely, on an iron stove. The early stove was an appliance of marked obduracy, a penal rockpile on which many a good country wife prematurely spent her beauty and strength. Kept burning the year round, it made one demand—dry wood—and delivered one temperature—very hot. Today's petulant complaint, "slaving over a hot stove," applies literally to the farmer's wife of the Victorian Age who required a placid temperament to endure the rigors of running a country house.

Laundry was the most physically punishing labor of the farm wife's routine. She tackled it once a week, normally in the yard, first lugging huge kettles of hot water from the kitchen or else building a fire outdoors for the same purpose. She had no machinery or "miracle" detergents—

Old-time fireplace cooking exposed housewife to searing heat and darting flames. It took skill to dodge these hazards and produce a meal.

only muscle power, a hollowed-out log that doubled as sink and scrubbing board, and chunks of homemade soap. The mountain of farm-filthy wash had to be reduced piece by piece, which meant hours of beating, rinsing and wringing before it fluttered triumphantly from the line.

The young country wife required stamina and fortitude equal to—perhaps even greater than—her husband's, and she soon acquired the callused hands, stooped back and careworn features that marked her station.

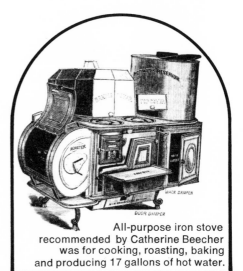

All-purpose iron stove recommended by Catherine Beecher was for cooking, roasting, baking and producing 17 gallons of hot water.

Mother, as we picture her, in all her bread-baking glory and well-starched neatness.

Mother, as she was, drudging and sweating from dawn to dusk to feed her family.

Frontier women stamped on the wash with their bare feet.

Strong man drags hot water from kitchen stove.

Housewives clobber laundry atop makeshift tub. Tennessee, ca. 1880.

Fresh Well Water?

The old wooden bucket delusion

The stone well and wooden bucket are romantic symbols of country life of the nineties, evoking nostalgia for the purity of spring water and derisive snorts at the chemical "manipulation" of modern tap water. However, our confidence in nature's ability to purify should be balanced by an appreciation of man's ability to pollute. The well water was indeed clean in the beginning, but the farmer inadvertently contaminated it.

For practical purposes the well was dug close to the farmhouse, which itself was close to the barnyard, stable, pigsty, coop and cesspool. With not even a pretense of drainage, the well was thus exposed to all sorts of noxious matter seeping through the ground. Slush from the kitchen, festering matter from privies, and seepage from animal wastes posed a growing danger to the water supply and filled the air with a vile odor.

A number of health experts warned that much of the sickness and unexplained "misery" of the country dweller could be traced to polluted wells, but they were ignored—even by some physicians. "I knew a doctor," said R. L. Dufus, "who had a cow-barn, a privy and a well all within one hundred feet of his kitchen."

In prairie regions and parts of New England where well-drilling was often unsuccessful, rain water was collected in garrets, barrels and underground cisterns. While not exposed to seepage contamination, it developed its own peculiar infestation from dust and flies.

The cities, meanwhile, were beginning to develop reliable, hygienically controlled water supplies for their own use. Between 1885 and 1892, New York spent $24 million to construct the New Croton Aqueduct. And it is not improbable that even as they drank their filtered water, many city dwellers expressed a longing for the "purer" product of a country well.

Congregating around barn yard pump, animals contributed to poisoning of wells.

Summer

Buzzing bugs never ceased to bleed man and beast

To the country dweller a hundred years ago swatting insects was an impractical solution to the summer invasion of flies, mosquitoes and their kin that turned the farmhouse into a buzzing, biting bedlam. In fact, there was no solution.

They swarmed through the open windows of the farmhouse, alighting on food and family, massing about the stove and ceiling, blackening fruit, wallowing in milk crocks and dying in the soup. During meals, boys were assigned leafy branches—"fly-shooers"—to help decrease the other diners' suffering. Night brought no relief as the detestable insects assembled in the bedrooms to plague the defenseless sleepers.

Russel Lynes said of window screening, introduced in the 1880's, that it was "the most humane contribution the nineteenth century made to the preservation of sanity and good temper."

Keeping windows open at night invited swarms of flies. Children fought the invaders in a losing battle.

Open milk cans attracted mosquitoes. Country milk stayed pure only briefly—if it ever was.

Winter

Smoking stoves or no heat at all

Before technology rescued them, it appears that the country people were faced in every crisis with a Hobson's choice. In summer if they opened their windows to avoid suffocation they were eaten alive by insects. And in winter if they closed the windows to avoid freezing they choked on smoky air.

The source of this winter indoor pollution was the iron stove, an inefficient little monster that glowed red-hot, sucked all the vitality from the air and replaced it with smoke. The preservation of heat being a higher priority in the house than proper ventilation, the farm family inhaled a harmful gas instead of the crisp country air that surrounded them.

On the prairie the scarcity of fuel made freezing in the rickety shacks and huts an ever-present danger. The floor was the frozen earth itself, and the only warm spot was the stove. During a blizzard it was not uncommon for the

Frontier wife collecting buffalo chips to use as fuel.

homesteader to bring the farm animals into his hut, and at times it became necessary to break up the furniture to feed the stove.

As Hamlin Garland summed it up: "Winter! No man knows what winter is until he has lived through a pine-board shanty on a Dakota plain with only buffalo bone for fuel."

Stoves, badly insulated, fumed—"the vilest annoyances incident to civilized living."

Farm children breathing poisonous air all night were said to wake up mornings in a state of moral insanity.

Bums

How safe was the countryside?

Scared farm wife gives
bum a sticky welcome.

In addition to the rural life's drudgery, there was a social menace—one which challenges a familiar assumption that the countryside was at least free of crime. The vagrant population posed a constant threat—bands of drifters and individual bums who lived by theft and begging. The nuisance showed no decrease toward the end of the century, when an official census put the tramp population at 50,000—an army larger than Wellington's at Waterloo.

While most of the tramps were not dangerous criminals, their outlandish appearance and mean disposition aroused fear in the farming communities they passed through. They formed a subculture that made people apprehensive—not for their scrounging or thefts of vegetables and underwear from clotheslines, but for the excesses they looked capable of. And this apprehension was not entirely groundless.

"From all over the East came reports of thefts, incendiary fires, rapes and even murders committed by vagrants. In some New England towns during 1877, people were forced to abandon their homes."

In our fascination with the sensational violence of the Old West we tend to regard the East of a century ago—especially the rural East—as crimefree. But that simply was not the case.

Suburban districts of New York and other towns were not considered safe for children unless the police protected them from wandering bums.

THE CONVOY ___ PROTECTION AGAINST TRAMPS,

TRAMP, TRAMP, TRAMP, THE TRAMP IS COMING!

Tramps, who "could give you a look to curdle milk," often terrorized
the countryside; they stole, caroused and sometimes committed murder.

Farm Children

They lead a life of mind-dulling blandness

"All work and no play makes Jack a dull boy" is an old saying that was curiously appropriate to farm children of both the frontier and rural East. From childhood the farmer's sons and daughters were routinely assigned multiple chores that filled their nonschool hours and limited their intellectual growth.

To envision the farm youngster's life in the Victorian period as one filled with carefree adventures is, therefore, a misconception. Apart from seasonal high points like the Fourth of July or a little sleighing in winter, their lives were modeled after their parents' lives—drudgery without end. While girls toiled along with their mothers—whose hardships were compared with those of oxen —boys toiled along with their fathers and trudged, at as early an age as ten years, behind their own plow team.

In general, the farmers' attitude to formal education was one of grudging concession, for they regarded the demands of school as depriving them of a free work force. And the schools closed in the summer months not for vacation but to enable young laborers to return full time to the land. "There just wasn't a minute to spare," recalls Millard F. Kennedy about his boyhood in Indiana, ". . . at nine or ten years of age I had so many chores to do that it seemed to my infantile mind that I practically ran the farm."

There was little about the early farm to inspire or satisfy a young mind. Lacking mechanical aids, the farms were crude, untidy places where broken carts and equipment languished in the fields, where "waste heaps filled the yard" and pigs had free range. Beyond learning to shovel dirt and shoe a horse, there was nothing to excite youthful curiosity.

"There was no chance to master the mechanical arts that a young man now needs to rise in life and give scope to his ambitions." The farm children were notoriously immature not as the result of an evil design but because the rigors of family survival made adult demands on their bodies and left their minds undeveloped.

Farmboy had no time for play till grimy work was finished.

Dull farm environment, and endless labors robbed farm children of rounded growth.

Young men were saddled with tasks that developed brawn but left the brain idle.

Hard Times

Mortgages— the worst of all weeds

In the 1880's, before the corporate farmers began erasing the horizon with money crops, close to 40 percent of the farmers were tenants, owning neither house nor land. The shabbiness of the property reflected the tenant farmers' debts, despair and lack of personal pride. Industrialization, which for the working class held at least the promise of prosperity, was the major cause of the decline of the family farm. Needing machinery to survive, farmers increased their debts to reduce pressure, and foreclosures drove these bewildered yet stoical people westward by the thousands. New England, especially, was stripped of its best men, who headed out apparently unaware that where they were going foreclosures were also approaching floodtide proportions.

The railroad monopolies, faithful to their calling, added to the trouble. Holding sway over the land, they seduced arriving farmers with lots on easy terms, only to hold them as ransom by charging outrageous freight rates on produce for market. The populist movement, starting in 1880 with the Kansas Revolt, was spawned by the farmers' anger at falling prices and widespread foreclosures. But it was a vain fight. They were absorbed in the end by what they feared most and understood least: the produce monopolies—agri-business in its infancy.

Signing the farm away.
Thirty percent of the farmers in the 1880s had to mortgage their land, overgrown with that worst of all weeds: debt. America was called a billion-dollar country —a billion dollars in mortgages.

Farmer mortgaged to railroads sees them gobble up his corn.
"Raise more hell than corn" was countermeasure
recommended by Elizabeth Lease, populist leader.

Foreclosure sales left farmers indigent—
a fate worse than that of city paupers.

Mother Nature

A wily mistress always ready to harass the frontiersman

There was little rejoicing for Western farmers who managed to remain independent as they faced periodic attempts by another and more violent force to repossess their property. Nature—particularly hostile on the frontier—put their durability to the test, and often won.

On the plains of Nebraska fierce winds filled the air with dust that penetrated houses, blew into eyes, nostrils, hair, and made walking a supreme effort—let alone doing chores. At times farmers were confronted with the heartbreaking task of resowing after acres of young plants had been uprooted in the fury. People caught in a Midwestern storm were transfixed by its fearful majesty, one observer recalling an electrical squall that caused "bolts of fire to jump from the horns of oxen."

Then, too, there were insect plagues that ravaged the land. (Such disasters are unlikely today because of cropdusting and pesticides.) Grasshoppers were a constant threat, as were the Rocky Mountain locusts, which in 1867 obliterated in a single day the whole of Dakota's harvest. A few years later they returned to strip the bark off trees, stopping trains cold as the oil from their crushed bodies made the locomotives' wheels spin. As if summoned by biblical prophecy, they would darken the Western sky with humming clouds, at times 150 miles wide by 100 miles deep.

The same wilderness that today is threatened by man threatened *him* a hundred years ago.

Prairie fires swept furiously across the plains. An 1869 Kansas conflagration lasting weeks proceeded on a 100-mile front, destroying everything in its path—farms, cattle, railroad stations, whole villages.

Grasshoppers visited the West in furious
onslaughts that could stop trains, destroy
a year's harvest in a day.

Iowa farmer tries to protect his
family from a tornado
by using a dugout shelter.

Cyclone threatens log cabin
with collapse.

Loneliness

The West was haunted by loneliness and its twin sister, despair

One aspect of the frontier has been dodged persistently to satisfy the vagaries of folk drama: the isolation and loneliness of families who lived there. There was no place lonelier than the frontier. The legal proviso that a homesteader stay on his claim—often extending for miles around—practically excluded human contacts. There was nowhere to go, no one to see; no casual visitors, no passers-by. The prairie itself, a bleak flat expanse unrelieved by so much as a single tree, emphasized the settlers' sense of physical separation from the human community.

Winter intensified their isolation, shutting them indoors for long periods and leaving them without even the meager comfort that the sight of another living creature might bring: "There is no bird life after the geese have passed on their way south. . . . The silence of death rests on the landscape, save where it is swept by cruel winds that drive through (the cottage's) unguarded apertures the dry, powdery snow."

The separation from neighbors and relatives was especially distressing; adding to the bleakness was the absence of an occasional

Settlers "live in the midst of a plain wider than the plains of Russia and must travel hundreds of miles to escape its monotony."

social event that would involve some happy commotion. There were only the dismal evenings, the endless drudgery and the restless behavior of cooped-up children, who were often prevented by bad weather from making the long trek to school. William Dean Howells describes how as a youngster he entertained himself by reading over and over again the old copy of a New York newspaper with which his father had wallpapered his cabin.

Frontier life was most depressing on those who by nature were gregarious. The sense of abandonment was most keenly felt by homesteaders who came from small European villages, where social gatherings and folk dances were a tradition, where life was hard but not lonesome. This sense of abandonment drove many settlers insane—especially the members of Swedish families. Proportionally the largest number of emigrants who ended up in asylums were of Scandinavian origin.

In our time it is a cliché to speak of the loneliness of the city, which is blamed for a variety of neuroses. But these are often the result of shallow relationships and the impersonality of urban culture. At least the city dweller is in touch with humanity, on however tenuous a basis; the settlers of the frontier, for months at a time, did not have even that little comfort.

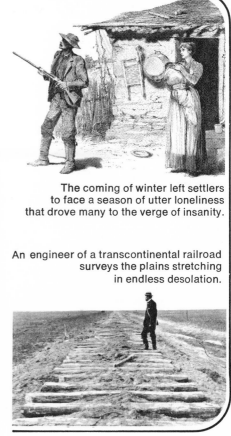

The coming of winter left settlers to face a season of utter loneliness that drove many to the verge of insanity.

An engineer of a transcontinental railroad surveys the plains stretching in endless desolation.

63

The Lure of the City

"Give me your rooftops and gas stoves and keep your acres of prairie."

The parents who endured farm life were not necessarily rewarded by the golden promise of a comfortable old age surrounded and supported by their farming children. As a rule the young hated the farm, its demoralizing hardships, its idiot monotony, its isolation, and as soon as they grew to independence—sometimes even before—thousands broke away from the land and settled in cities large and small.

Girls especially, sharing a mother's toil and witness to her premature disfigurement, were vehement in their prejudice. Frederick Law Olmsted was told by a young woman in 1870: "If I were offered a deed of the best farm . . . on the condition of going back to the country to live, I would not take it. I would rather face starvation in town."

No matter what the conditions in workshop and factory, they seemed more bearable than the slavery on a farm. The pay, modest as it was, exceeded what could be earned on the land, and even after long working hours one's life was one's own. There was the excitement of new companionships and experiences, the satisfaction and maturity that come with self-reliance, the diverse possibilities a city offers, in Olmsted's words, to "nourish the juices of life." There was also the increased prospect of romance and, for the incorrigible dreamer, the chance of wealth and eternal happiness.

The big cities offered endless opportunities for success, and equally many for failure. Advice to the young immigrants warning them of the lures and pitfalls that awaited them was largely ignored. Young men who lacked the cunning and hardness to compete descended to menial work and sometimes to crime. Many girls who believed the city would solve their problems of boredom and isolation ended up as sweatshop seamstresses, many as prostitutes.

Even before the Civil War and through the 1880's, and despite their many squalid features, the large cities were magnets that attracted great numbers of rural and small-town people. It was a great American exodus, thousands upon thousands of the disillusioned streaming cityward.

Restless farm boys dreamed of the city and its more intense life.

Many farm girls,
lured by the city's glitter,
found their hopes betrayed:
the desolation of the farm
was replaced by the
drudgery of the sweatshop.

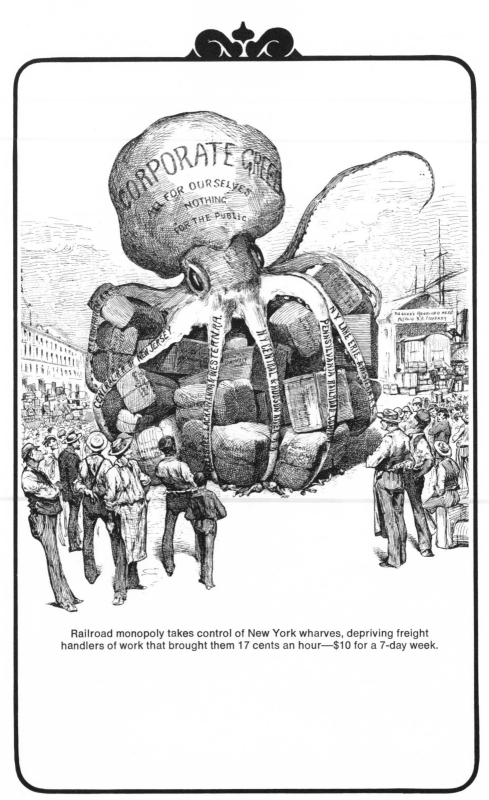

Railroad monopoly takes control of New York wharves, depriving freight handlers of work that brought them 17 cents an hour—$10 for a 7-day week.

5 Work

HISTORY OFFERS A YARDSTICK by which to measure the status of the American worker. Today he has dignity and protection; less than a hundred years ago he was poor, debased and unprotected. Industrialists of the period regarded labor as a commodity—a raw material like ore or lumber to be mined of its vitality and flushed away. Profits were enormous against meager wages—"Never before have the rich been so rich and the poor been so poor"—an imbalance that helped 1 percent of the population by 1890 to own as much as the remaining 99 percent put together. Marshall Field's income was calculated to be $600 an hour, while his shopgirls, at a salary of $3 to $5 a week, had to work over three years to earn that amount. Virtually unopposed by any organized front—by 1900 only 3.5 percent of the work force was unionized—employers hired and fired at will. A New England shoe manufacturer sacked outright all of his workers and replaced them with Chinese laborers he brought from the West Coast who were willing to work for $26 a month. To survive in the absence of social benefits, workers endured wretched conditions. The huge labor pool, augmented by a massive influx of foreigners, created a rivalry for even the most repugnant jobs. And if labor unrest caused an occasional stir, industrialist Jay Gould was confident he had the solution for it: "I can hire one half of the working class to kill the other half."

Working Conditions

"The laboring man in this bounteous and hospitable country has no ground for complaint."

It is apparent from this statement that Chauncey Depew never put in a 12-hour shift on the floor of a steel mill. Unless, of course, he enjoyed working in 117-degree heat in a smoky, clangorous bedlam for a maximum of $1.25 a day. Or perhaps he was attracted by the laborers' hovels and their 7-day workweek.

Conditions that were attended by constant danger, that had destroyed the health of thousands by age forty, were inspired less by malice than by the entrepreneurs' holy pledge to keep the cost of labor down—at any cost—which meant to keep the people down. Coal mines and iron and steel mills, the primordial industries, were especially brutal on their manpower because of the constant pressure exerted on them by every other industry.

Entrepreneurs viewed the worker as part of the great cogwheel of industry.

In the mills two shifts worked round the clock at a demonic pace, which faltered only at shift changeover. Shorter work periods, with their added pauses in production, were never considered. The economist J. G. Brooks quotes a mill foreman who admitted that the machines were deliberately set at the utmost speed a human could endure: "It is a pity that men have to work like this, but there is no help for it. The machinery drives us at a gallop."

Exposure to the infernal heat and poisonous gases endemic to their work shattered many steelworkers' physique prematurely. Of these individuals, the unlucky ones were sacked and the lucky ones were demoted, with a concomitant wage reduction from $1.25 to $1 or less a day. Aged workers were given jobs as sweepers or submenials, preferring to labor 12 hours for 75 cents than face a pensionless retirement.

Steel mills had no monopoly on serious health hazards. There was the sawdust of factories, the stone dust of quarries, the toxic emanations in chemical plants, and the coal dust in the mines. The miner, it was said, "went down to work as to an open grave, not knowing when it might close on him." Usually the son followed the father, starting as a breaker boy at age six, and often entering manhood stunted from the effects of early employment.

Iron puddler, stripped to waist
and exposed to suffocating gas and smoke.

Miners had to spend days crawling through
shafts filled with coal-gas and dust.

Their eyes exposed to metal grindings,
workers polish safes.

Long-handled ladle used for pouring steel
forced the worker into a twisted posture.

Accidents

"If you accept a job, you must accept its risk."

The headlong excesses of domestic industry were reflected in an accident rate that moved President Harrison in 1892 to observe: "American workmen are subjected to peril of life and limb as great as a soldier in time of war." In his classic book on poverty, Robert Hunter put the yearly total of killed and injured at one million, a higher number in proportion to the labor force than in any other nation.

Aside from the steel mills the railroad industry was the most lethal to its workers, killing in 1890 one railroader for every 306 employed and injuring one for every 30 employed. Out of a work force of 749,301 this amounted to a yearly total of 2451 deaths, which rose in 1900 to 2675 killed and 41,142 injured. It should be noted that these casualty lists cover only railroaders in the line of duty: civilian casualties in

Unprotected powershafts maimed and killed hoopskirted workers.

The miner: "Gas hurls us to eternity and the props and timbers to a chaos."

train collisions and level-crossing accidents were another matter. The *New York Evening Post* concluded that the deaths caused by American railroads between June 1898 and 1900 were about equal to British Army losses in the three-year Boer War.

In the high-risk job category the circus stuntman and test pilot today enjoy greater life assurance than did the brakeman of yesterday, whose work called for precarious leaps between bucking freight cars at the command of the locomotive's whistle. In icy weather, it often became a macabre dance of death. Also subject to sudden death—albeit to a lesser degree—were the train couplers, whose omnipresent hazard was loss of hands and fingers in the primitive link-and-pin devices. It took an act of law in 1893 to force the railroads to replace these man-traps.

Industry's cavalier attitude to safety had a predictable effect on lower-echelon bosses. One railroad-yard superintendent refused to roof a loading platform, even though in the cold his men had contracted rheumatism and asthma. His observation: "Men are cheaper than shingles. . . . There's a dozen waiting when one drops out."

Whether a worker was mutilated by a buzz saw, crushed by a beam, interred in a mine, or fell down a shaft, it was always "his own bad luck." The courts as a rule sided with the employer; in any event, few accident victims or their kin had the money to bring suit. Companies disclaimed responsibility, refused to install protective apparatus, and paid no compensation. Their only concession to human life was to pay for burying the dead!

Brakemen often fell as the train curved or came to a sudden stop. Balancing on icy roofs was railroading's most hazardous job.

Victim of an accident, a worker on the Pennsylvania railroad is forced to return to the job to sustain himself. Workmen's compensation was unknown.
PHOTO COURTESY OF A. M. SCHAPPER

Sweatshops

"A slavery as real as ever disgraced the South."

There was one industry in the Gilded Age where sudden death and maiming were not occupational hazards, but where, instead of this luxury, the alternatives of exhaustion or starvation were offered. This was the garment industry, and at its heart was the sweatshop.

Manned largely by newly arrived immigrants who had landed with high hopes and little cash, the sweatshop ran from factory-size hall where men and women slaved under regimental supervision to the informality of a squalid room with an entire family engaged in piecework. The sweatshop operator, called "sweater," shrewdly exploited the need of work and shelter by offering the newcomers a package deal: against an initial "key payment" of $5 he stuffed them into a slum and subcontracted work to them for a pittance.

In New York's Lower East Side —the center of the industry—it was commonplace to find whole families working through the night merely to subsist. With rents $8 to $12 a month and living costs per individual a minimum of $5 a month, a garment worker could not support a family solely on his own pay. Consequently his wife—and children—were sucked into the grim cycle of working and sleeping.

At the risk of his health a man could make $9 to $10 a week for pressing and delivering new garments to the wholesaler; a woman, $7, for the punishing job of seaming three dozen shirts. The standard wage for a girl was $3 to $5, which, according to the head of the Women's Protective Union, Mrs. M. W. Ferrer, yielded her no more than a loaf of bread, a cup of tea, and a bed in a tenement attic. When asked how the sweatshop girls could live, she said, "They can't."

Sweatshop owner browbeats seamstress. Fines were imposed for talking, smiling, breaking a needle. To reach their quota, girls had to put in an 84-hour week at a wage averaging 5 cents an hour. Working pace hardly left time to eat or sleep.

Garment carrier.
Lithograph by Jacob Epstein, made
when he was beginning his career
on New York's Lower East Side.

increased as families grew. The humanitarian Robert Spargo recalls an interview with a mother of four whose husband's greatest efforts brought home no more than $6 per week. "It's awful," she said, "I must work, else we get nothing to eat and turned into the street besides. . . . Often we go to our beds as we left them. Cooking? Oh, I cook nothing, for I haven't the time."

While *Cosmopolitan* magazine observed that sewing in a sweatshop was "the most grinding oppression that can be practiced on a woman," it was not the most dangerous occupation. There were the soap-packing plants, for instance, where girls were exposed to caustic soda that turned their nails yellow and ate away at their fingers. There were the flower-making workshops where arsenic, liberally applied to produce vivid colors, wrecked the appearance and health of thousands of girls with sores, swelling of the limbs, nausea and, often, complete debility.

Bread and tea formed the staple diet of the sweater's victims, to whom even the preparation of beans was a costly and wearisome task. And the pressure to produce

"Eat? Who has time to eat? Tea and a piece of bread is all we have time for. Sometimes you want to swallow the teapot."

The cities of the Gilded Age had an excess of these plants, and twelve hours a day in their toxic atmosphere left their mark on workers for life.

But nothing compared with the hazards and indignities of the tobacco "in home" factories. Here, for a meager income, women and children were forced to endure the most sickening exhalations as they stripped the leaves. *Harper's Magazine* described the effects of endless hours of this work: "Their eyes are dead, a stupor overcomes them, their nerves are unsettled and their lungs diseased in almost every case."

If tobacco stripping was the nadir of sweatshop employment, then the sewing room of A. T. Stewart, New York's greatest retailer of the 1870's, was perhaps its zenith. Here was to be found a thin layer of civility, and air that was relatively clean. But Stewart ran his two thousand workers with an iron hand, assessing fines against latecomers and those who misdirected bun-

Twenty cents a day.

dles. Hours were from 7:30 A.M. to 9 P.M., and sewing girls received $3 a week—a notoriously low salary even then. Bathroom facilities were inadequate—perhaps deliberately so, in order to keep the needles humming—and this proved a menace to the health of young girls who endured discomfort when men were

Young tobacco strippers, exposed to air that would make the most inveterate smoker sick. "Tobacco is everywhere—children delve in it, roll in it, sleep beside it. The dust seasons their food and befouls the water they drink."

Sewing room in department store of A. T. Stewart, who was said to be "as tender to his employees as a fireman is to his truck."

around rather than run the gauntlet in humiliation.

Although Stewart was criticized for regarding his workers as mere "cogs in the ... machinery of his establishment," he was more widely acclaimed as a man of impeccable honesty whose sewing room was a model of decent employment practices.

Young women functioned as conveyor belts in store and factory. Cashgirls at $3 a week complained that they were "box-carrying machines."

Spindle boy in Georgia cotton mill. Small children had to stand on boxes to reach the spools which whirled without a break. Children's hands could be caught and badly hurt. "If you speak, they say, 'Get out.'"

Child Labor

"We take them as soon as they can stand up."

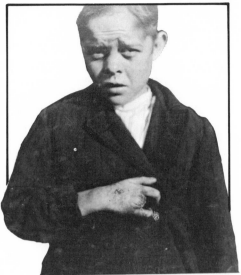

Ruined for life by an accident, child workers received no compensation. Upon receipt of $1, parents released the company of claims in case of injury. Charitable employers made one-time $5 payment to an injured child.

Not only did they take them, as the Southern manager said in reference to children working in his factory, but running machines late at night they were sometimes kept awake "by the vigilant superintendent with cold water dashed into their faces." "Late" meant two o'clock in the morning in upstate New York, where "mere babies" were found employed in a cannery. In their utter weariness after work, these children often forgot their hunger and fell asleep with food in their mouths.

Child labor was not just a sporadic manifestation of Victorian cold-bloodedness, it was a widespread practice encouraged by industry, agreed to by parents, and generally ignored by government. For employers the tiny workers were a bargain at $1.50

Philadelphia factory boys demonstrate for better pay and time out for school. Once employed in a factory, schooling ended for most boys and condemned them to a lifetime of menial labor.

Trapper boys, paid 25 cents a day, worked 12 to 14 hours in dark, air-swept shafts.

Breaker boys crouched as they picked slate from newly broken coal moving on a conveyor belt. Their hands bled from sharp stones; coal dust ruined their lungs; "like old men," they had a permanent stoop. "You begin in the breaker," the miners said, "and end up at the breaker, broken yourself."

to $2.50 a week, and, besides, they claimed that factory work was good for the little devils; the Puritan Work Ethic prevailed against the "sloth of children, their idleness by which they are corrupted."

Less culpable perhaps were the poor parents, who were seduced into giving their assent at the prospect of reducing their struggle even by so small a margin. And many children appeased their parents' conscience by fancying factory over school, which by law they had to attend fourteen weeks a year to become eligible for work. Sometimes child laborers—and their parents—would lie about their age to obtain employment. In fact, children in Syracuse, New York, in 1904 were heard to complain, "The factories will not take you unless you are eight years old."

Whatever the circumstances, the little workers got no special favors. Their hours were as long and their conditions as grim as those of an adult. Some textile-

mill boys were so small they had to be raised on boxes to service the twirling spindles, their hands in constant danger of being caught. Young mine workers, exposed to poisonous dust and injury, earned 25 cents for a 12- to 14-hour day.

There were opponents of child labor, among them charitable institutions, but they proved powerless. A law had been passed as early as 1842 by Massachusetts —always a leader in humanitarian causes—that confined the workday of children under age twelve to ten hours. But this state and others with similar statutes lacked the means to enforce them. With an estimated 6 percent of its child population engaged in factory work in the 1880's, New York State had only two industrial inspectors. Under such sparse surveillance, the "importing" of child labor went on freely. Children were transported from Tennessee, where a prohibitive law was in force, to South Carolina, where none existed. "Little chil-

Boys labored as glass factory workers from 5 p.m. to 3 a.m., "disappearing into the night." As molder boys they replaced men, who found the work "too hot."

dren from seven to fourteen years of age [were] shipped like cattle or hogs."

An 1870 census put the total of child workers at 700,000, but this did not include the thousands who worked city streets as vendors, messengers and shoeshine boys. Child labor actually grew threefold in the South in the decade from 1890, increasing the national figure in 1900 to 1,752,187.

One third of all mill employees were children. They also worked in tobacco fields, canneries and mines; in meatpacking, hosiery, silk, wool, hemp and jute mills. Finally, in 1904, the National Child Labor Committee was formed and began its vigorous campaign to protect the coming generation.

"The golf links lie so near the mill
That nearly every day
The laboring children can look out
And see the men at play."

Standard of Living

"Steady work? Nothing steady but want and misery."

To most workers, the miseries of employment were more acceptable than the alternative: unemployment. Layoff—a constant threat—meant ruin, and the bands of tramps that menaced the countryside during the depression of the 1870's included decent men who were merely jobless and in despair. The crisis year of 1877 saw an estimated two and a quarter to three million men unemployed. In the depression of 1893–98 the total was four million—almost one out of every five workers. In the absence of benefits or relief of any kind, many families had to sleep in police stations.

Ruin followed loss of work because what came in on Friday was gone by Thursday. And contrary to popular belief, $2 a day in the 1870's was not a lot of money. Except for New Yorkers, rents were lower, taking only 10 to 15 percent of an average wage (for dismal accommodations), and certain foods could be bought reasonably. But statistics show that food absorbed 50 percent of low incomes.

In 1882 a Boston bootmaker with a family of five and $660 yearly income spent $120 on rent, $319.29 on groceries. Measured against $2 a day, an acceptable wage, the average prices per pound—butter, 19 cents; bacon, 10 cents; fowl, 10–15 cents; and eggs, 15 cents a dozen—were quite high. Many families had only $1 a day to spend—a desperate hardship. "They often live on bread alone and have no meat for weeks."

Through a larcenous scheme, workers were forced to pay higher food prices in company towns. Wages were mostly in scrip, redeemable only in company stores that charged inflated prices. In the coal regions of Pennsylvania a barrel of flour that cost $6.50 in a "cash" store was $8.50 at the company store; butter at 19 cents was 25 cents in scrip, and so on. Workers who protested this extortion were not only sacked but evicted from their homes, which the company also owned.

The refusal to accept wage cuts led to lockouts, lifted only after the workers pledged not to join a union.

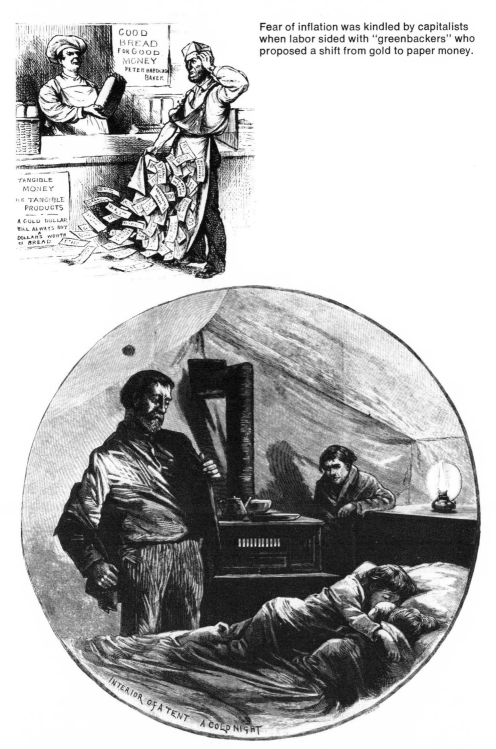

Fear of inflation was kindled by capitalists when labor sided with "greenbackers" who proposed a shift from gold to paper money.

Striker's family, expelled from company dwelling, seeks refuge in tent—a far cry from Carnegie's dictum: "The American workman should be appreciative of all the refinements of life. His home must be the most artistic."

Strikes

"We struck . . . because we were without hope."

To most people of the upper classes, crowds of angry men in shabby clothes—no matter what their cause—were always wrong. No matter that they were workers driven to the wall by the practices of their employers. No matter that their families were hungry. No matter that they were infuriated by wage reductions while profits were rising.

In the face of such total blindness to legitimate grievances, violence was inevitable. Between 1881 and 1900 American labor staged 2378 strikes involving more than six million workers. With few exceptions, such as the railroad walkout against Jay Gould in 1888, these strikes proved calamitous to the workers' cause. The powerful industrialists, taking refuge in the respectable sanctuary of "law and order," controlled public opinion and slandered the labor movement as a seditious form of conspiracy. Strikes were blamed on "blatant anarchists," "socialists," or "hordes of untrained immigrants yet unfamiliar with the institutions of the Republic."

No doubt there were some ruthless agitators within the rank and file, not to speak of roughnecks who welcomed mob rule, but labor hardly needed such incitement. It was already charged to the brim by abuses and economic hardship, and it struck only as a last resort. For instance, the great railroad strike of 1877 was called to protest a 10 percent cut in wages. Regrettable brutalities occurred along the line, but the men could hardly be blamed for

The Great American Scarecrow. The public blamed Communists for inciting strikes.

resisting the plunder of their starvation pay. Militia bayonets forced the workers to give in.

The Pullman strike had a similar origin and outcome. Pullman, who ran his company towns with the authority of a medieval lord, had instituted five reductions in wages between May and December 1893, the last one amounting to almost 30 percent—all this notwithstanding the fact that the company had about $25 million in its coffers, with a distribution of $2.5 million in dividends for 1891.

The Homestead steel strike of 1892 was generated by Henry Clay Frick himself with the admitted intention of breaking the union he hated. More than twenty died in the subsequent uprising, which was crushed by five thousand militiamen and led to the dismissal of three thousand workers. These strikes, an observer noted, achieved "nothing but heightened police power—and the erection of great armories across the land" to have troops

Labor's acts led only to suppression by armies hired to "stem the awful tide of socialism."

ready should "anarchists" dare to interfere with the orderly conduct of business.

The attitude of the authorities toward strikers, in fact toward any manifestation of mass disgruntlement, was exclusively punitive, and the public at large agreed with this approach. Henry Ward Beecher, gentle, unctuous brother of Harriet, who had held many antislavery meetings in his church, said of strikers: "If the club of the policeman, knocking out the brains of the rioter, will answer, then well and good; but if it does not promptly meet the exigency, then bullets and bayonets, canister and grape ... constitute the one remedy. ... Napoleon was right when he said the way to deal with a mob is to exterminate it."

Pullman striker assailed by militiamen.

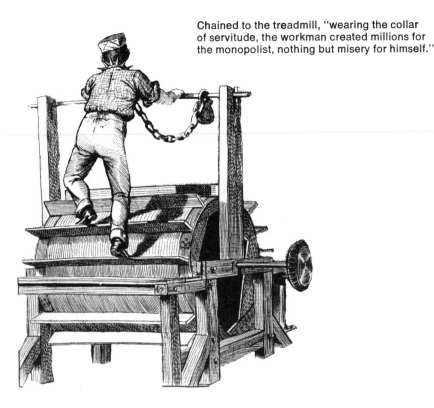

Chained to the treadmill, "wearing the collar of servitude, the workman created millions for the monopolist, nothing but misery for himself."

Technology

"The demon which is destroying the people"

Mankind's attitude toward the machine has always been ambivalent. What Edward Bellamy called "the soulless machine, incapable of any motive but insatiable greed" was feared by the workers, many of whose jobs would not have existed without it. Particularly bitter were former artisans—shoemakers, handworkers in iron, wood and stone—whose crafts had been absorbed by mechanization. They felt debased working in factories at repetitive tasks a child could perform, their fine skills exchanged for the relentless rhythm of the machine.

The early trade unions, immersed in the old craftsmen's philosophy, warned workers of the day when giant robots that made human labor expendable would chase them from the factories. They watched with fear the installation of new machinery, though they did not go as far as the Luddites, the English machine smashers of the early 1800's.

Countering this widespread alarm, however, was the view of several far-sighted economists that the factory system produced more good than evil, "that the machine does not rob of work but gives more employment" by its constant proliferation of new industries providing new jobs.

The dehumanizing aspects of the assembly line are still hotly proclaimed, even though it has increased workers' prosperity and leisure time. In his book, *The Doomsday Syndrome,* J. R. Maddox asks: "... who now afflicted by technology would willingly settle instead for the life of a Victorian laborer ...?"

The answer could be that the machine is merely nuts and bolts; we do the dehumanizing all by ourselves.

The Demon which is destroying the People: cartoon of 1882 propounds Frankenstein theory of mechanization: workers are doomed to be replaced by robots.

The Nemesis of Neglect

There floats a phantom in the slum's foul air
Into the spectre of that loathly lair
Red-handed, ruthless, furtive, unerect
'Tis murderous crime—the nemesis of neglect.

6 Crime

THE LAWLESSNESS of the 1860's through the 1890's, wrote criminologist Cesare Lombroso "is an American phenomenon with no equal in the rest of the world." Statistics of the period—if not entirely reliable—appear to substantiate his claim. In this period the crime rate rose 445 percent against a population rise of 170 percent. Dominating the record was, of course, the West, where the gun-happy barbarity was damned by observers both foreign and native for producing a "great dismal swamp of civilization." The lawlessness of the cities was less romanticized, but its perils were even greater to the common citizen.

New York was known as the world's center of crime, earning the title with an extravagant toll of murders, assaults and robberies. And these were not confined to the slums that were their primary breeding ground. The business and residential areas became infested with burglars and muggers who were after spoils richer than what their own neighborhoods offered. "Each day," *Leslie's Weekly* observed in 1868, "we see ghastly records of crime . . . murder seems to have run riot and each citizen asks . . . 'Who is safe?'" Many thoughtful citizens looked with shame and alarm on their era. And it was neither hysteria nor sensationalism that compelled the *Charleston News and Chronicle* to state: "Murder and violence are the distinguishing marks of our civilization."

Street Crime

"We have to rid ourselves of this incubus of evil."

George Templeton Strong, who lived in the Gramercy Park area of New York City, noted in his diary in 1857: "Most of my friends are investing in revolvers and carry them about at night." He added an account of nightly robberies that took place near his home and described "nocturnal fears of assault" as a city tradition. By 1870, however, street crime had greatly increased, and with it the public's sense of helplessness.

The suspicion of strangers that characterizes the New York personality is no quirk of fate; it developed, as did the porcupine's bristles, in a predatory environment. In Wood's *Illustrated Handbook* of 1872, visitors to the city were warned to beware of all "who

New York policemen assaulted in battle with criminal: "The history of American cities since the Civil War is the history of lawlessness."

accost you in the street." A good general rule was to avoid walking late at night anywhere "except in the busiest thoroughfares." Central Park was considered unsafe after sundown, and if a stranger wished to visit a dance hall he was urged to go armed or with a policeman.

The lack of well-lighted streets added to the danger. A threatened gas strike in 1873 alarmed New Yorkers. "Even with the streets lighted, assaults and robberies are frequent," wrote *Harper's Weekly,* "in total darkness crime would hold high carnival. . . . Every dwelling house would have to be converted into a fortress."

Street crime was a greater menace in Chicago, where the murder rate had quadrupled in less than twenty years. Muggings were commonplace, even in daylight, and the criminals were usually tougher than in the East. George Ade recalls that in his early Chicago days (or nights) he made it a rule "to use the middle of the street so that no hold-up man could step from an alley and salute us with a piece of lead—or an elongated canvas bag filled with sand." His re-miniscences are hardly discredited by Chicago's 1893 arrest ratio—one arrest for every eleven residents. There were eight times more murders in Chicago than in Paris.

The criminal element was not entirely professional. Owing to the absence of laws against concealed weapons, any drifter or drunk who got hold of a pistol became a menace. Although his object might have been only to sneak behind a counter to rifle a till or to filch a coat from a hallway, the outcome often was bloodshed.

Street crime remains a major problem in American cities, but with public awareness and increased police efficiency there is at least reason to believe that it will not remain so. Less than a hundred years ago—before the advent of telephones and squad cars—the public mood was one of unflagging pessimism.

The Gay Nineties saw assaults increase in number and intensity— "from barbarism to vile brutality."

Juvenile Delinquents

"They have no occupation and learn no art but to steal."

The streets of New York became a school to turn little toughs into major outlaws. Gangs proliferated during the age—the Gophers, the Dead Rabbits, the Molasses Gang, to mention a few—and the "first act of pilfering to the second of burglary was as regular as the progress of a schoolboy from class to class."

Physical training, so to speak, was acquired in gang warfare or in the terrorization of a neighborhood, which the youths would usurp with the imperiousness of lions. Some gangs could muster up to a thousand before sallying forth "on their mission of pillage and death." Particularly ruthless were the flashy New York Bowery Boys, whose territory no policeman would enter without a partner—and then only during the day, never at night.

If the streets were schools for crime, the prisons were graduate colleges. Here youthful offenders were thrown together with hardened criminals, whose corrupting influence complemented the courts' general indifference to reform. Judge Ben Lindsey recalls his assignment as a young attorney to look after two prisoners. His clients turned out to be young boys who had been

Mother pleads for mercy. Once a juvenile offender was caught, his fate was sealed by exposure to the brutality of prison and reform school.

locked in a cell for sixty days with a safecracker and horse thief ". . . upon whom they had learned to look as great heroes."

Like grownups, children were locked up on the slightest suspicion of misdeed. In Chicago "upwards to 10,000 young persons were arrested, clubbed, handcuffed, and jostled around . . . without having committed any crime." Such excesses nurtured in the young a disrespect for the law that strengthened the inclination toward delinquency.

Juvenile outlaws progressed from ruffianism to murder "like schoolboys moving from class to class."

Youthful desperado arraigned before judge. Before juvenile courts were established, wayward children were treated as adult offenders.

Youths in prison: unconcerned, as though incarceration was an everyday event."

Police!

"Our last prop is the cop."

To modern city residents, particularly to those who must travel alone at night, nothing is more reassuring than the appearance of a policeman. Despite widespread complaints about police corruption, there appears to be confidence that the cop will do his public duty. In the good old days, such confidence was largely absent.

The job requirements for policemen were rudimentary. Toughness was necessary to meet the challenge from the underworld, but to enlist the bully type of aspirant, ethical deficiencies often had to be overlooked. The behavior of these cops—which ranged from minor graft-taking to covert alliances with criminals—generated public mistrust of policemen at large. Undoubtedly there were brave, conscientious

Benevolent onlooker: policeman calmly twirls his stick as mugger does his stuff.

Men in blue come to blows. Battle flared in 1858 between city-controlled municipal police and metropolitan police appointed by Albany "because city was unable to govern itself."

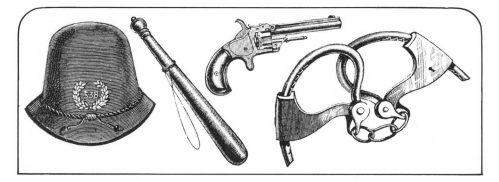

men in the ranks, but the forces' reputation was earned by the great number of police who were inclined toward brutality and always eager for a handout.

Appropriately, the New York police force—or "police farce," as contemporaries called it—started with a riot. In 1857 the State Legislature, convinced that the city was "too corrupt to govern itself," fired all the municipal policemen, who were under city jurisdiction, and attempted to replace them with a new metropolitan police force under an Albany-appointed commissioner. Mayor Fernando Wood refused to surrender his authority over his men and, finally, the two forces clashed in a pitched battle in front of City Hall. With the help of the 7th Regiment State Guard the state won, and Wood had to give in.

However, the nature of the department changed little over the ensuing fifty years; in fact, if anything, it changed for the worse. Police appointments were political, and party considerations usually took precedence over character qualifications. Nor did public mistrust recede. Chronically undermanned and lacking the technology to respond swiftly to crime, the police became the butt of unceasing criticism. People in trouble agreed—more in despair than in jest—"Our last prop is the cop."

The policeman's hatred of the public was heartily reciprocated. Most people thought of them as ruffians who constantly guzzled free beer.

New York's Own Swingers

"There is more law in a policeman's stick than in a volume of Supreme Court decisions."

In his enforcement of the law the old-time cop seldom gave the impression of being an assiduous student of the Constitution, which grants the police only limited powers. To him, the club personified the law, and he used it with relish on suspects, drunks—whom he thought little of killing if they resisted arrest—even persons in orderly crowds; in fact, he used it to dispense "instant justice" on whomsoever he deemed in need of it.

In 1894 the Lexow Committee, in its investigation of police practices, charged that the station house frequently became a form of slaughterhouse "where prisoners purportedly under the law's protection were brutally kicked and maltreated—almost in sight of the judge presiding in the court." Rookies were reprimanded when they brought in evildoers "unmarked," since it was normal procedure to give arrestees a beating so the cop would "have some-

What first strikes the stranger on arriving in New York.

thing to show in court."

Always keen to advance their cause, the police took advantage of the complete news blackout on their activities to juggle statistics and make New York appear to the world a "low-crime area." The commissioners never informed the public about countless assorted crimes. "How many hundred things that trench powerfully on comfort transpire daily under the very noses of these guardians—which they do not see or are powerless to prevent!"

Conditions were similar in other cities. The police forces were not professional organizations but political ones, and efforts to change this were futile. In Chicago the Pinkerton Agency offered to take over the police at two-thirds what the city already was spending on an ineffectual force, and to guarantee that "the citizens would actually be protected." But nothing came of it. Police work, with all its chances for kickbacks and protection money, was too good a business to let go. Burlesque sketches invariably presented the cop as a bully or villain, and a search of the record indicates why.

A full-fledged policeman emerged after thirty days' instruction in the use of a nightstick.

Graft

"Police colluding with scoundrels, coddling villains they are set to watch"

Graft in the old days was not merely a fringe benefit for the police; it was for patrolman and chief alike a cardinal value by which they measured their livelihood. At the higher level there was a well-established bureau-

The police force was suspected of having a hand in the $3-million robbery of Manhattan Savings Institution in 1878. Even Inspector Byrnes, an imperious figure in New York police history, was not above suspicion—the Lexow Committee found that on a salary of under $10,000 he had amassed a fortune of $350,000.

cracy handling payoffs received from two sources: legitimate business, for "nonharassment"; and organized crime, for protection. Graft made it possible for New York's vast criminal society to flourish and for the police to profit in millions of dollars. "It was a charge rarely denied that our police captains are in collusion with the keepers of dance houses and gambling houses of every sort. They receive from these, stipends larger than their yearly salaries."

The system proved impervious to reform movements. A Society for the Prevention of Crime, founded in 1878—the year of Boss Tweed's death—had no effect until the Reverend Charles Parkhurst became its head. In 1892 Dr. Parkhurst, an intense Presbyterian minister, devoted a firebrand sermon to Tammany-backed crime in New York in which he denounced the politicians and, by implication, the police, as "a lying, perjured, libidinous lot." Rocked by the accusations, Albany issued immediate denials and the district attorney slapped a summons on Dr. Parkhurst requesting that he prove his charges.

The clergyman, accompanied by a private detective, promptly went to the crime-infested Red Light district where he exposed the profound depth of police corruption. The subsequent public outcry led to a bill for an investigation that was vetoed by the governor. However, two years later, in 1894, under mounting public pressure the Lexow Committee was formed.

The testimony assembled by this committee proved the fearful abuse of police power; it proved the lavish extent of graft extorted from thousands of businesses, from pushcart to steamship company; it established that jobs in the New York Police Department could be bought at a definite scale of prices—from $100 for a patrolman to $1500 for a captaincy; it revealed that almost all police transactions were subject to financial appraisal: "From the rookie's first involvement with the department he was made aware of the systematic and pervasive impact of bribery."

Corruption so institutionalized appears, in retrospect, to somewhat mitigate the evil of the individual. If the police could make bootblack Frank Martine cough up $100 for the exclusive franchise to clean shoes outside their own station house at 67th Street and Third Avenue, they could have felt no guilt. It was simply their way of life.

Dr. Charles Parkhurst in disguise ready to probe New York's red-light district. His escort detective Charles W. Gardner is at his left.

Prostitution

"Anybody who denies that licentiousness in this town is municipally protected is either a knave or an idiot."

The Victorian posture was one of stern resistance to human weakness, in particular to carnal pleasures. But the business of vice was extensive enough in the cities of the 1880's to suggest the devil was not in limbo. Respectable standards prescribed laws against prostitution in varying degrees of stringency, but these were largely unenforced as the more urgent demands of lust and money proved irresistible.

In the larger cities such as New York, Chicago, San Francisco and New Orleans, prostitution entrepreneurs offered services for all classes and pocketbooks, from palatial bagnios and brownstones to dives in the slum areas. It was a commercial trade, practiced with remarkable openness. The stock solicitation "Hello, dear, won't you come home with me?" astounded visitors to New York, where the girls were especially brazen. Dr. Parkhurst was himself accosted there, in a Water Street den, by a prostitute "caked with dirt . . . with the brashness that a Grand Central hackman asks you to have a cab."

Sex had become a commodity; as America's first woman doctor, Elizabeth Blackwell, observed: "Shrewdness and large capital are enlisted in the lawless stimulation of the mighty instinct of sex." Police protection cost the bordello operator an initiation fee of $300 to $500 and $30 to $50 monthly thereafter, traditionally collected by the precinct captain.

The enormous number of girls involved provided an interesting counterpoint to the proclaimed rectitude of Victorian life. In 1870, when its population was 950,000, New York City had an estimated 10,000 prostitutes; in 1890, the figure given by Police Commissioner Byrnes was 40,000.

Prostitution's unsavory side effects were often more damaging than the vice itself, as the bordellos attracted and encouraged all manner of criminals, who found in them a harvest of easy victims.

Under the squinting eye of a cop, an Episcopal minister (visiting New York) is lured into a "den of iniquity."

Working the Elevated:
"Man-fishers along New York's Sixth Avenue
play siren tricks to rope in transient trade."

"Temples of Lust" often proved
traps in which the pleasure-seeker
was robbed of his belongings.

Spoilsmen and Plunderers

"Government by politicians, of politicians, for politicians"

Judged even by today's practices, which are undistinguished by virtue, politics in the good old days was thoroughly corrupt. Criminal influences dominated government, and politics became, in Ambrose Bierce's phrase, "the conduct of public affairs for private advantage." Although the federal government was mortified by an occasional scandal, the political corruption expressed itself most arrantly at the municipal level, where scoundrels plundered "that fruitful and ill-fenced orchard: The City Treasury."

Hindsight makes it lamentably clear that key municipal offices, rather than being forcibly seized by these manipulators, were in fact abandoned to them by decent individuals. Herbert Spencer saw the danger to American democracy in 1882 when he warned of the widespread "acquiescence to the wrong ... the readiness to permit trespassers." Professional men were too selfish to become involved, and intellectuals like Henry Adams were no match for the unconscionable bullies whose only aim was to help themselves to public funds.

The most outstanding example of these rogues was New York City's Boss William Tweed. His political headquarters, Tammany Hall, was later described by the Reverend Parkhurst as "not a party" but "a business enterprise like Standard Oil and Western Union." It has been estimated that during its reign the Tweed Ring robbed the city of $160

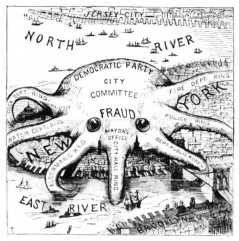

New York's Tammany octopus.

million, which compares favorably with the losses of the Chicago fire—put at $30 million. No services reached the public without first being submitted to a thorough pilfering. Every important city job was twisted into a sinecure for some political trickster, whether it was the post of police magistrate or that of municipal commissioner. Crespy tells of the case of a man brought back from a distant state to answer for a felony who ended up in New York as the auditor of public accounts. Favors were for sale in any department. "Manipulators thought no more of buying an alderman than going out and buying a watermelon."

Other cities during these decades were being subjected to similar boss rule. Chicago had

The Lexow Committee declared in 1894: "Honest elections have no existence in New York."

its Nash machine; Boston its Lomasney ring; and Kansas City had Pendergast. From 1867 to 1922 the Cameron-Quay-Penrose dynasty owned Philadelphia, a city Lincoln Steffens reported was so corrupt that a man he knew who was writing a book on the abuses that prevailed during the building of City Hall had run out of space after three volumes. It was Steffens, too, who called St. Louis "the worst governed city in the world."

The bosses maintained control by diligently currying favor with the "little people," to whom they appeared as heroes from their own social class who protected them from the tyranny of the rich and powerful. There was always the glad hand, the free liquor, the little gifts of cash and coal, the job for a new immigrant and hasty naturalization. "Every good man takes care of his friends," pronounced George Washington Plunket, who fully expected that in the next election they would vote for him "early and often." Such subtle pressures made "reform" a dirty word, and there were times when reasonable men doubted whether a majority of its residents really wanted their city to be cleansed of evil.

Bosses defied reform of city charter. Reigning absolute, they found "politicking more profitable than thieving."

President U. S. Grant takes leave of White House friend, War Secretary W. W. Belknap, accused of accepting kickbacks.

The Law

"No one respects the law . . . no one respects the courts . . . the courts don't respect themselves."

This sad verdict on justice was handed down by a journalist in the 1880's, and any overstatement therein appears to have been only marginal. Lower-court judges were men of low caliber whose conduct of trials was influenced by their appointers—the bosses—the very elements they were supposed to control. Once the boss had interceded with the stock plea, "Your Honor, I have known this boy for years. He works hard to take care of his old mother," the young tough with a criminal record was assured to go free.

It was widely believed that these same judges—merciless on the poor defendant with no friends—would never convict a rich man, that the rich could and did, literally, get away with murder. In this climate it was not

The Power behind the throne of Justice.

surprising that boss-protected gambling and liquor and vice operations were carried on with impunity. Large corporations tampered openly with the courts, paying off judges and juries alike without any sense of misdeed. As Collis P. Huntington, that "man of impeccable dishonesty," put it: "If you have to pay money to have the right thing done, it is only just and fair to do it."

Certificates of insanity could easily be had to "legalize" burglary, arson, or murder.

Jay Gould controlled the city because he controlled its courts. It was said of him that he could commit a murder without fear of arrest or conviction.

The Mafia already made its power felt in the 1890's, when it terrorized the New Orleans court charged with investigating the Mafia gang murder of that city's chief of police, David Hennessy. A brash and courageous crime-buster, Hennessy was hated by the Mafia for deporting Giuseppe Esposito, gang leader on the New Orleans waterfront.

The Crime of Punishment

"Great walled cages with rows of inmates shuffling past in close array"

Penal philosophy in the latter half of the nineteenth century did not advance with technology. Prisons were strictly for punishment, which was carried out with medieval excesses. Public opinion as a whole supported this view, and criminals customarily were treated as a subhuman species. Even the compassionate Jacob Riis approved of the "beating up of young toughs," but his was a mild recommendation compared with what was actually practiced. Starvation, floggings, chainings and torture were blandly routine.

Although prison reform did have some devotees, and isolated experiments in rehabilitation had been carried out—notably in the Philadelphia and Auburn systems—unyielding repression was the rule. The Tombs prison in New York City, with its heavy Egyptian-style architecture, symbolized the penal code for one observer: [it] "fairly represented the fact that American prisons are more Egyptian than Christian and worthy of a pharaoh." And Governor Blackburn of Kentucky compared his state's prisons to the Black Hole of Calcutta.

However, the very abyss of inhumanity was to be found in Southern prisons, where Blacks were singled out for special brutalities. "Men are chained in iron collars; a boy of fourteen sentenced to five years for only being in a whiskey shop where a man was killed wears handcuffs . . . they have cut into his wrists."

Owing to the corruption and incompetence of the court system, the prisons housed many who were either innocent of crime or mentally deranged. And upon these unfortunates penal barbarity had its most crippling impact.

Sing Sing prisoner under deadly cold water shower. Guards' personal spite was frequently the reason for such punishment.

Labor gang convict compelled to wear an iron crown.

Beatings were administered on the flimsiest provocation, often crippling the prisoner for life.

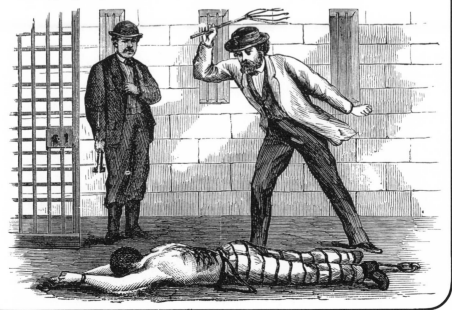

Lynching

"What are the atrocities of the Inquisition compared to those of the lynching mobs among us?"

Perhaps the darkest stain on the history of the United States—a nation that sanctified itself in the rule of law—was the lynching epidemic of the late nineteenth century. According to the *Chicago Tribune,* between 1882 and 1903 no less than 3337 people died in these outrages. And it is sobering to consider that many of the victims were totally innocent of any crime; proven guilt was inconsequential when mass hysteria lusted for blood.

Two instances epitomize the madness that possessed the lynch mobs. On February 22, 1898, a black man named F. B. Baker was lynched at Lake City, South Carolina, for accepting the office of postmaster. In 1893, in Paris, Texas, a Black kidnapped by lynchers was publicly burned at the stake with extreme torture while women and children helped kindle the flames.

State authorities showed criminal neglect in their tacit approval of lynch law, and in 99 percent of the cases no arrests were made. Despite this, the mass of Americans felt lynching to be the crime of the century.

What was even more shameful was the fact that lynching participants confessed to no feeling of guilt. To them, incredibly, it was justice.

"The blackest period for the black people."
Between 1882 and 1903, lynchings of blacks totaled 2,060.

Negro lynched for the alleged rape of a white woman in Beekly, West Virginia.

Jewish immigrant in cellar dwelling ready for his evening meal:
bread and tea. Photograph by Jacob Riis.

7 Food and Drink

THERE IS A BENIGN NOSTALGIA for the food of the Gilded Age, reinforced no doubt by the proliferation of old-fashioned cookbooks crammed with mouth-watering recipes. The cornucopia comes to mind as neatly symbolizing America's blessed fertility which lured the half-starved Irishman across the ocean. Culinarily speaking, America appeared to be one gigantic, groaning board.

But the board in reality groaned only for a small minority of Americans. The country's fertility notwithstanding, the masses were forced to subsist on a crude and scanty diet of which tea and bread were staples, supplemented now and then by a soup or stew of questionable origin. Ragpickers and fellow paupers ate what they could find in trash cans, and many people shopped for their dinner at the secondhand food market—a feature of large cities—where they could select from leftover groceries and cast-off trimmings and bones from butcher shops.

With lack of hygienic standards, the established purveyors in the slum districts—from street vendor to corner grocer—sold food that would not today be considered fit for human consumption.

Nostalgia even for the food of most rural Americans cannot survive the light of truth. While to a degree substantial, their diet was very simple, monotonous and often far from healthful.

Beware!

"food approaches a condition of putridity"

Before the rise of the meat-packing industry, beef reached the cities "on the hoof," shipped live from the West in slow trains. The cattle that survived the journey in the packed rail cars arrived so emaciated and maimed that their drovers had to prod them with pointed steel rods to keep them on their feet. The final stop was the slaughterhouse—an extravagant formality, it seemed, for beasts that were about to succumb to starvation.

These conditions made it difficult even for the rich to buy fresh viands. *Harper's Weekly* complained in 1869: "The city people are in constant danger of buying unwholesome meat; the dealers are unscrupulous, the public uneducated." The poor, meanwhile, had to settle for the cheapest cuts, which often were decayed.

In the absence of electric refrigeration, perishable goods were subject to the whims of the weather. Meat and fowl for sale were simply hung on racks or placed on market counters. The New York Council of Hygiene reported in 1869 that the foods thus displayed "undergo spontaneous deterioration ... becoming absolutely poisonous ...

One is tempted to believe that with meat and fish so unreliable the urban Victorians sustained themselves by consuming an

Cattle, half starved and emaciated after a long trip, are weighted for sale to slaughterhouses.

Poor people bought from hackmen, who offered discards from uptown stores. House-wife applies smell test to suspect fish.

New York policemen chasing after butcher's cart loaded with decayed "bob veal."

Market stalls laden with fowl.
"Fresh" chicken and turkey
were exposed to the air for days.

Smoked meats, dried fruits and fish lay open to New York's dusty air,
"a health hazard to the unwary buyer."

abundance of fruit. But that was not the case. They had a lingering suspicion of fruit—and vegetables —that had its origins in a cholera epidemic of 1832 which was believed to have been caused by fruit. In fact, following the epidemic, the New York City Council had forbidden the sale of all fruits, and though the ban had been lifted some years later the mistrust was to remain.

Bought by the grocers in green condition so that it would remain salable for a longer period, the fruit—instead of ripening attractively as they had hoped— rotted on the counters. *Harper's Weekly* in 1872 complained that in markets throughout the city there were cartloads of decayed fruit such as bruised oranges and rotten bananas "to partake of which was almost certain death."

"Decaying fruits and vegetables are daily entombed in the protuberant stomachs of thousands of children whose pallid faces are the familiar attribute of childhood in the slums."

Milk

A water shortage would put the milkman out of business.

It was common knowledge to New Yorkers that their milk was diluted. And the dealers were neither subtle nor timid about it; all they required was a water pump to boost two quarts of milk to a gallon. Nor was that the end of the mischief: to improve the color of milk from diseased cattle they frequently added molasses, chalk or plaster of Paris.

A diseased cow, unable to stand, is pulled up to be milked. Distilleries kept a stable of such animals, fed them mash and whiskey slops. The milk made babies tipsy and often sick.

114

No wonder, that in 1889 New York's public health commissioner reported seeing in certain districts a "decidedly suspicious-looking fluid bearing the name of milk."

Bacteria-infected milk held lethal possibilities of which people were unaware. The root of this problem was in the dairy farms, invariably dirty, where the milch cows were improperly fed and housed.

It was not unusual for a city administration to sell its garbage to a farmer, who promptly fed it to his cows. Or for a distillery to keep cows and feed them distillery wastes, producing what was called "swill milk." This particular liquid, which purportedly made babies tipsy, caused a scandal in the New York of 1870 when it was revealed that some of the cows cooped up for years in filthy stables were so

City visitors wait for "farm-fresh" milk.

enfeebled from tuberculosis that they had to be raised on cranes to remain "milkable" until they died.

When in 1902 the city's Health Commission tested 3970 milk samples it was found that 2095, or 52.77 percent, were adulterated.

The New York City Health Board managed at times to catch purveyors of watered milk. In 1902, the Rockefeller Institute reported that half of all New York milk was diluted. Dairymen, it was said, cheat as meanly as faro dealers.

Butter

"An unpardonable enormity"

Dairy by-products, it appeared to the Victorian manufacturers, provided a fine opportunity to improvise; here imagination was needed, not scruples. And the butter they produced demonstrated a remarkable talent—not for making butter but for making money. Selling in the 1880's for a respectable average of 19 cents a pound, it was often rancid, and

Grocers presented "sham butter" as a creamery product, but it came "from the dead hog, not the live cow."

Unsavory raw materials used in "bogus butter" manufacture spread a penetrating stench through New York streets.

either a mixture of casein and water or of calcium, gypsum, gelatin fat and mashed potatoes.

The alternative was "bogus butter," and the ingredients of this concoction were so wildly incongruous as to generate several investigations by city and state. Fat from hogs along with every conceivable animal part that the slaughterhouses could not turn to cash were picked up by the oleo makers and processed in filthy worksheds. Bleaches were blended into the mix to give the product the appearance of real butter.

A margarine factory employee in 1889 told New York State investigators that his work had made "his hands so sore . . . his nails came off, his hair dropped out and he had to be confined to Bellevue Hospital for general debility." That customers frequently bought this pestilent muck and fed it to their families was due to the artfulness of the grocers, who scraped off the real labels and relettered the boxes "Western butter" or "best creamery butter."

Things are seldom what they seem;
Skim milk masquerades as cream;
Lard and soap we eat for cheese;
Butter is but axle-grease.

Adulteration

"The cupidity of the food manufacturer is not a petty swindle, it is a crime."

Adulteration of foodstuffs was conventional practice among the bakers and grocers of the 1880's, who met the growing food demands of city residents by extending their raw materials with a variety of questionable additives. The bakers—never noted for cleanliness, and historically obdurate to public criticism—stretched and preserved their dough with doses of alum and sulfur of copper. Customers were continually enraged to discover chunks of foreign matter in their loaves, such as oven ash and grit from the baker's machinery.

The national craving for a cup of really good coffee was just as intense as it is today, though the chances of brewing one were incalculably smaller. A report of the 1870's suggests why. "How complacently we receive from the hands of the grocer a package of 'pure Java'—which is not Java at all but only a mixture of roasted beans and peas, flavored with the ever-present chicory and rye."

When it came to candy, to which adults were addicted almost as much as children, the ingredients were notably harmful.

Candy could not be made attractively colorful without the addition of strongly toxic substances. The resultant sweets "on which the children nibble all day long" contained elements that were markedly dangerous—the degree of harm depending on the health of the consumer and the amount eaten.

The expansion of food canning

Bakers were chastised for adding alum to flour and for letting grit fall into the dough.

Candies gaily colored contained toxic chemicals.

raised hopes that spoilage—which caused uncountable deaths—would be conquered. But the side effects of canning should have been predictable. Only the cheapest varieties of foodstuffs were canned, and chemicals added to prevent decay didn't always work: "The jar of pickles upon your table contains an acid so powerful and so fatal to health the pickle becomes a soft mess that crumbles to the touch." At least in the "fresh" food market one could smell a fish. But who could smell beforehand what was inside a can?

The widespread distrust of "tinned food" was vindicated in later years by the Embalmed Beef Scandal, which revealed that U.S. soldiers during the Spanish-American War were fed from tin cans containing decayed meat. There were even claims that the cans had been left over from the Civil War.

With all food suspected of adulteration, *Puck,* the comic weekly, suggested that diners "test before they eat."

Children's Food

Beer and sardines for the babies—pickles for the boys

Slum children scavenging for food in an ash barrel.

Reflecting upon what it had to endure, one is impressed by the ruggedness of the Victorian stomach. But what of the children—especially the poor children—and their tender insides? Many of them "had not ever eaten a mouthful of wholesome food." Pushed onto the streets to beg and pick rags, they foraged for the rotten discards from groceries and restaurants. And whatever few cents they did make were spent on foods that played havoc with their stomachs.

Many children developed a strange hunger for pickles, generated, Robert Spargo believed, by chronic underfeeding that caused a nervous craving for some stimulant—much like the craving of an alcoholic for liquor. But the deterioration went further. "It is a horrible fact that many children whose diet is so unwholesome cannot eat decent food even when they are hungry." Slum children at times refused to touch passable food offered them during outings arranged by charitable groups. Some of them had to be taught to eat: it took days before they could be induced to touch eggs and drink milk and give up their pickles.

How some people live:
a second-hand meat saloon
on Alaska Street, Philadelphia.

Eating Habits

"Americans don't eat — they gobble, gulp, go."

In the preparation and eating of food, American custom in the late nineteenth century kept faithful pace with the crudity and haste of industry. Except in rarefied circles, people did not practice artful cuisine or etiquette, which were regarded as incompatible with the no-nonsense sentiments of a bullish nation. *Harper's Magazine* observed of contemporary cooking habits ". . . we are indifferent to a degree that is almost criminal . . . If you pass out of the narrow range of millionaires, you find a superabundance of bad, hasty cooking, indigestible hot bread, tough beefsteaks, greasy potatoes."

Impatient waiters forced eaters to race through dinners. Restaurant fare tended to be massive but carelessly prepared. "There is abundance to satisfy a cyclops—but hardly anything to eat."

Consider, too, that this fare was eaten at flank speed, whether at home or in a restaurant. Americans, it was noted, "take their food as if it was part of their work," displaying great impatience to get it over with. In an 1856 article, "Why We Get Sick," *Harper's* described a businessman rushing through dinner "where ten to one he is clinching a bargain . . . between bolted beef and bolted pudding." Waiters loyal to ritual often served all dinner courses simultaneously, goading the diner to speed up his "wolfing," so he could finish his soup before the entrée went cold.

Foreigners were greatly amused by the American office sign, "Out for lunch—back in five minutes," which neatly suggests the atmosphere of the standard eating place: "The clatter of plates and knives, the slamming of doors, the bellowing of waiters are mingled in a wild chaos—everybody talks at once, orders at once, eats at once."

The same circuslike scramble prevailed in the boarding houses, where a long reach increased the inmate's chances of survival. Dickens described the reduction in ten minutes of a heap of food to a few scraps "as if a famine were to set in tomorrow morning."

Foreign dignitaries deplored high-speed eating and feeding: "A pitiless hospitality—a genius for overdoing it." One victim, after eating an extra-large oyster, felt he had "swallowed a baby."

Five-minute lunches were the butt of foreign travelers' jokes.

"Who can expect greatness from a nation of moody dyspeptics?"

The Hungarian writer Vay de Vaya held the opinion that for a regimen calculated to injure the stomach, teeth and general health, no one could surpass the Americans. Whatever the clinical definition of stomach distress, it provided a gold mine for the patent-medicine makers, who might as well have advertised: "We will help your stomach digest any food properly. You do the eating—we'll do the rest!" Despite criticism, the market burgeoned. It appeared that the dyspeptic was here to stay, "growling and groaning by turns through life, a burden to himself and a bore to his friends."

When the bell sounded, the boarding-house inmates rushed to the dining room for a marathon of guzzle and grab.

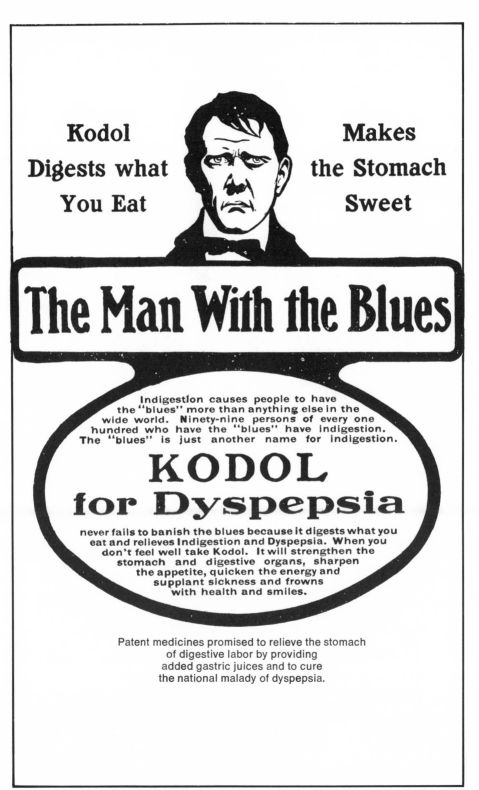

Kodol Digests what You Eat

Makes the Stomach Sweet

The Man With the Blues

Indigestion causes people to have the "blues" more than anything else in the wide world. Ninety-nine persons of every one hundred who have the "blues" have indigestion. The "blues" is just another name for indigestion.

KODOL for Dyspepsia

never fails to banish the blues because it digests what you eat and relieves Indigestion and Dyspepsia. When you don't feel well take Kodol. It will strengthen the stomach and digestive organs, sharpen the appetite, quicken the energy and supplant sickness and frowns with health and smiles.

Patent medicines promised to relieve the stomach of digestive labor by providing added gastric juices and to cure the national malady of dyspepsia.

The Western Diet

Hog and hominy— the diet of proverbial ignominy

For many pioneers the pipe dream of ready-to-eat frontier hogs ended in bitter disillusionment.

The staff of life in the West can be described with laudable brevity: corn. Easily cultivated on the frontier, corn kept the pioneers from starving and enabled them to push onward; without it the Great Migration, some believe, would have taken a hundred years. But although it yielded sustenance, corn did not provide an adequate diet, even if more than thirty-two ways were contrived to prepare it in the form of bread, hominy cake, pudding— whether it was boiled, roasted, mashed or popped. Eaten three times a day, seven days a week, the frontier family's diet would cause a riot in today's penitentiaries. The children, especially, suffered from the lack of fruits and vegetables, except for seasonal greens like dandelion, pigweed, buffalo peas and sheep sorrel, which did not add up to a sufficient amount of vitamins to promote growth or prevent scurvy.

During her stay in the South, Harriet Martineau compared corn to gold: "The man who has it has everything; he can sow the land with it, and for the rest everything eats corn, from slave to chick." Corn also helped raise the second mainstay of frontier life: hogs. They provided meat the year round, and their fat was used as a substitute for butter. But apart from its desolate monotony, the pork and biscuit diet often was injurious to health, as 6.3 percent of all pigs were infected with trichinosis.

Frontier baby sucking on bacon rind suspended on string to prevent swallowing. Mothers were too busy to give affection and time to children, who were raised "like corn and cattle."

Lacking bread, pioneer miners became expert flingers of flapjacks. Made of cornmeal, they tasted "like disks of red flannel."

Pioneers were sustained by corn, which could be planted in the woods even before stumps were cleared. Fed on a steady diet of corn and salted hogmeat, children suffered from vitamin deficiency and developed scurvy and scrofulous sores.

Frontiersman-bachelor has meal in make-shift kitchen. Fruit and vegetables were rarities in the West before the plows turned the plains.

A FAMILY BITE.

Drinking

"Dramshops yawn at every step."

The drinking habits of Americans in the good old days paralleled their eating habits: both were frenzied and excessive. Although never a notably sober people, their drinking developed during the period to become a national menace, the per capita consumption of alcohol rising from 8 gallons in 1878 to 17 gallons in 1898, reaching in that year the staggering total of 1.25 billion gallons. The temperance movement grew correspondingly, and its zealous crusade compelled a number of states to go dry. But its influence was more theatrical than actual, as it made no noticeable impact on the upward curve in the statistics of drunkenness.

The causes of heavy drinking were both ethnic and social. Each successive group of immigrants appearing in the cities carried its own bottled tradition, whether it was the German addiction to beer or the Irish fondness for malt liquor. Dismal living conditions and loneliness magnified their thirst, and the liquor that was a gratifying indulgence for the rich became for them an inescapable crutch. To the poor the downtown saloon, no matter how squalid, was a warm refuge from habitations that the *New York Graphic* in 1874 described as "unfit for horses or swine."

The flourishing bar trade in the slum districts of every major city was a model example of the supply-and-demand theory in practice. In New York, Chicago, Philadelphia and Boston, "dramshops yawned at every step." It was estimated in 1880 that for every hundred of its male inhabitants, New York contained one saloon. (The national average in the same year was 1:735.) They outnumbered churches ten to one and schools twenty to one. Jacob Riis counted 111 Protestant churches below 14th Street against 4065 saloons, and in the neighborhood of Jane Addams' Hull House there were 9 churches and 250 saloons; the Chicago average was 1:300. Judging by these odds, the maxim "Wherever God builds, the devil builds next door" paid an unintended tribute to Satan's propensities.

However, the devil's success was in no small measure due to his alliance with the politicians, who allowed saloons to proliferate in gross violation of the licensing laws. For here was the fulcrum of their power—the simple exchange of booze for votes—indeed the direct route from barroom politician to alderman or state senator. For the same reasons, closing-hour ordinances existed only on paper. George Ade tells us there were saloons in Chicago that had not closed their doors for years.

With few exceptions the old-time taverns could be graded only in degrees of squalor. Jacob Riis noticed in the worst of them that dogs were unable to stand the atmosphere and fled into the street. George Ade describes a typical saloon, a mill-town shack in Pennsylvania where a half-naked iron-puddler gulps down—after a 12-hour shift—an enormous hooker of straight rye, "each heroic wallop followed by a tall glass of beer as a chaser."

A repeated symbol of the Gilded Age is the elegant bar of New York's Hoffman House. But a more accurate symbol would be Demon Rum and its dispensaries.

Bibulous Back Country

"Liquor proved as powerful an aid to communications as printer's ink."

For the city dweller who visited his country relatives, the bleak prospect of forced abstinence did not exist. Whether New England farmers, Western settlers or nomadic cowhands, they were sure to have a supply of liquor, or at least be in close proximity to one. Nor was alcoholism an epidemic peculiar to cities alone; when it came to strong liquor, country folk proved just as susceptible.

On the frontier, the indispensable fixture of a town was the saloon, where drunken brawls and gunfights were far more savage than in Eastern cities. Notable among our Western heroes was an alcoholic murderer—Doc Holiday—hired to clean up Tombstone, Ariz., by Wyatt Earp, himself a former bar bouncer. The importance of alcohol on the frontier may be gauged by the number of "whiskey towns" that grew around liquor stores. Often located close to Indian reservations, where alcohol was outlawed, these towns flourished, as in the case of Lexington, Okla., around a single trade—drinking.

Even the Western farmer, often pictured as the very model of virtue and temperance, was subject to heavy drinking, the victim of his own mash. With corn and rye in abundance and markets far removed, he found it considerably cheaper to convert the grain into liquor—at a cost of 20 cents a barrel—and transport it in reduced bulk. His temptation to imbibe was sharpened by a lonely, hostile environment and, in the brutal winters, to have an attractive confederate against the cold.

Everyone indulged: "men, women and children, preachers and church members as well as the ungodly." Besides Scripture, liquor was a source of inspiration for some Baptist ministers, whose sermons often were nothing but

Warning against drunken driving was given in this 1880 temperance lecture slide.

alcoholic tirades. New Englanders, like other rural Americans distilling their liquor from the most abundant local crop, ineluctably became addicted to cider, and to its more potent essence, applejack. Horace Greeley, a teetotaler, maintained that in New Hampshire a family of six or eight consumed a barrel of cider a week. At this rate the graduation, or descent, to alcoholism was simplified: "The transition from cider to more potent stimulants was easy and natural, so that whole families died drunkards and vagabond paupers . . ."

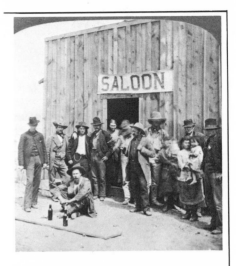

The saloon formed the nucleus of many Western settlements, which grew into "whiskey towns."

Whiskey readily distilled by farmers from their crop of corn proved ruinous to many households in both East and West.

The Saloon

"An institute of vice"

The effect of alcoholism on both the victim and his family is well known, but in the Victorian period it had an even more profound, more hopeless impact. There were no social agencies or privately sponsored clinics to help the alcoholic; there was no real understanding of his compulsion. He could turn to only one place for commiseration, for relief, even for food: the saloon.

The drunkard's wife was an object of deepest tragedy. Cast into despair by a lack of love and seeing her husband's earnings disappear, her suffering was increased by fears—often realized—that in their poverty and demoralization the children would follow in their father's path. A woman in the slums of Chicago told Jane Addams: "You might say it's a disgrace to have your son beat you up for the sake of a bit of money you've earned scrubbing, but I haven't the heart

"Liquor and beer was sold to anyone tall enough to hook his chin over the counter." Children brought pitchers to be filled with "beer for Father."

to blame the boy for doing what he's seen his father do all his life; his father forever went wild when the drink was in him and struck me to the very day of his death."

Child alcoholics were not uncommon, having developed an early taste for drink as the result of constant trips to the bar to have a pitcher filled with "beer for Father." From her bed in New York's Presbyterian Hospital,

Drunkenness was branded as the cause "of nine-tenths of misery of the working class" by T. Powderly, of the Knights of Labor.

Forsaken drunk faces nightmare of delirium tremens.

young Lucie Zucheriechi lisped, "Give me whiskey, a little drop of whiskey, and I will give you a kiss." Carried thence from a slum, she was an alcoholic, dying of cirrhosis of the liver.

When it came to the quality of his drinks, the alcoholic got less— or more perhaps—than he paid for. Liquor was "in its majority a vile compound," often pure alcohol with some coloring added and a fancy label, sold as genuine whiskey, brandy or rum. Beer was spiced with adulterants and had a high alcoholic content to keep it fresh, causing, it was observed, riotous scenes "as if murder was about to be committed." Many saloons offered free lunches, making their foods "saltier than the seven seas" to ensure that the drunks would remain thirsty— and inside.

Ultimately, the human wreckage caused by alcohol ended either in the hospitals, where the victims died in a rage of delirium tremens, in reformatories such as Ward's Island, N.Y., or in prison. In 1870, 60 percent of New York City's prison inmates were found to be drunks. The Committee of Fifty, a group of citizens studying the effects of alcoholism, were alarmed to find that out of 13,402 convicts they examined, 50 percent were alcoholics, and that liquor was at least a determining factor, if not always the "sole cause of their crime."

Summarizing the problems of alcohol during the Gilded Age, it is startling to note that the per capita consumption was somewhat less than it is today. But several factors render the comparison largely invalid, among them the social drinking of modern women; the rigid supervision of distilleries, breweries, and the bar and package trades; the widespread partiality toward moderate use; the successful rehabilitation programs for alcoholics. In the old days such an enlightened climate did not exist, and the result was liquor abuse of unmitigated horror.

In New York drunks were confined in the Asylum for Inebriates on Blackwell's Island. Released after a few days of abstinence, they often went on a new binge and, incarcerated again, became known as "rounders."

Yellow Jack (fever) pawing its way into U.S. cities, finding a
fertile breeding ground in garbage-strewn streets. Since Pilgrim
days this "American plague" posed a constant threat.

8 Health

THE TECHNOLOGICAL ADVANCES of the Gilded Age were not accompanied by corresponding advances in medicine; health care remained dumbly neglected. "Where were the medical equivalents of the steam engine or the telegraph?" asks Richard H. Shyrock, one of our leading medical historians. True, it was the age of Pasteur and Lister, but it took decades for their discoveries to affect public health. Meanwhile, endemic diseases fed by the dirt and overcrowding of cities ran their course, and a people growing accustomed to electricity remained frightened by the threat of smallpox, (although preventable since the discovery of vaccination by Jenner in 1796) diphtheria, typhoid and yellow fever.

Epidemics were attributed to the "Miasma," some unknown intangible effluvium that crept into the air, and whether rich or poor, one could be well of a morning and dead that night. New York's compassionate health commissioner, Dr. Stephen Smith, described the panic when a cholera epidemic was imminent as paralyzing the commerce of the whole city, even the whole nation, and causing a mass exodus among the more prosperous.

But perhaps the most distressing feature of old-time medicine was its inability, outside of surgical anesthesia, to alleviate pain. Even minor afflictions often meant weeks of suffering that a modern society, accustomed to instant relief, would not have the fortitude to endure.

Urban Epidemics

Yellow fever rips the South

To Americans before the turn of the century the origin of yellow fever was unknown, but the effects were only too visible; its victims literally turned yellow and died in agony. The Memphis epidemic of 1878 took 5150 lives. Many of the sick had crawled into holes "twisted out of shape," their bodies discovered later "only by the stench of decaying flesh." *Leslie's Weekly* described the suffering of an entire family caught in one room, the mother dead "with her body sprawled across the bed . . . black vomit like coffee grounds spattered all over . . . the children rolling on the floor, groaning." Out of a population of 38,500, 20,000 deserted the city.

New Orleans was struck in the same year, a predictable circumstance to many who believed it to be the most unhealthy city on earth ". . . a dungheap . . . Its streets . . . saturated with the oozings of foul privy vaults." At the height of the epidemic in September the death rate reached a hundred a day; funeral processions were about the only traffic to be seen; and an "indescribable doom" pervaded the city. But the total dead, estimated at 3977, was only half that of the 1853 epidemic, which had taken 7848 lives.

Known also as the American Plague, since it had struck the Bay Colony in 1647, yellow fever decimated Philadelphia in 1793, thus ending its supremacy in the young Union. In the Spanish-American War, soldiers were more fearful of this disease than of bullets.

Appropriately, the disease was stamped out by an American, Dr. Walter Reed, an Army surgeon, who in 1900 with a team of heroic assistants traced its source to a virus carried by the *Aedes aegypti* mosquito and thus eliminated—almost at a single blow—one of the scourges of mankind.

Curfew to prevent spread of contagion.

Burning of disinfectants was futile measure.

Makeshift hearses conveyed dead bodies.

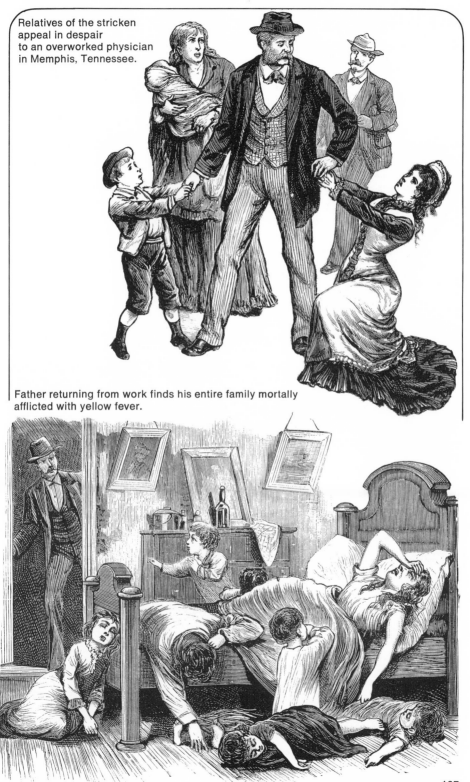

Relatives of the stricken appeal in despair to an overworked physician in Memphis, Tennessee.

Father returning from work finds his entire family mortally afflicted with yellow fever.

137

Disinfection and Quarantine

Half-measures to stem the epidemic tide

The struggle against disease during the post-Civil War period took two forms: the rational and the theatrical. In the first case, scientists—many at great personal risk—experimented doggedly to isolate the causes. In the second, public health officials splashed disinfectant about the slums to demonstrate vigorous action against pestilence—a measure that proved to be more a public relations gesture than a success in improving sanitation.

Because it was the major gateway for immigrants, New York was the most vulnerable to epidemics, and outbreaks—albeit not major ones—continued to occur despite the convocation of an imposing Board of Health in 1867. Instead of being served by professional sanitarians, the

Boss Tweed welcomes cholera to city streets as well prepared for epidemic as anything in Asia.

public was at the mercy of so-called health wardens, political appointees of impressive ignorance. Asked to define hygiene, one of them declared, "It is a mist rising from wet ground." Confining their "health" measures to daubing the garbage-filled streets with carbolic acid and chloride, the wardens shrank from entering any slum dwelling suspected of contagion on the excuse that "the breaking up of

Cholera-prevention box subjected the traveler to the ineffectual fumes of lime and carbolic acid.

A ship with cholera suspects was attacked off Fire Island, New York, to forestall landing.

these dens and fever nests only scatters the pestilence."

The real cause of epidemic disease—the microorganisms bred in the garbage—was not understood and dyphtheria, scarlet fever and smallpox flourished, spreading from the slums to cleaner and less crowded areas. No city dweller was immune from tuberculosis—known as the "white plague"—which was accepted as a form of divine affliction. Even as late as 1899, when a pioneer in bacteriology, Dr. Herman Biggs, declared it a preventable disease, he was sharply rebuked by the New York Academy of Medicine.

Another measure employed to prevent the spread of epidemics was the quarantining of immigrant ships flying the yellow flag, the international signal of epidemic aboard. Authorities refused to let these vessels land, and often passengers—following a strenuous voyage—were confined to the hold for many days until the contagion appeared to have subsided. In 1892, after 981 immigrants had been designated to land on Fire Island for further quarantine, they were met by "a mob of a thousand brutal citizens . . . many of them with arms . . ." For two days they were subjected to "every imaginable horror" until the National Guard was called out to see that they landed in safety.

Although one can sympathize with the authorities' position in applying it, quarantine did not stop cholera and was futile against yellow fever, which was transmitted through mosquito bite. An ordeal for travelers, importers, and ships' personnel, quarantine was merely a gesture to show easily panicked city dwellers that their government was concerned about safeguarding public health.

Dousing filthy streets and homes with disinfectants proved ineffective and a waste of money. The stench was merely replaced by the pungent odor of carbolic acid.

Frontier Health

"Malarial fever caused more anguish than the threat of scalping Indians."

Thousands of Westward-bound pioneers took with them the illusion that no matter how tough it turned out, frontier life would at least be healthful and free of the epidemics that plagued the East. However, they also took along the germs to destroy that illusion. Smallpox traveled with them to break out in towns and even on the thinly settled prairies.

In swampy frontier regions, the settlers' strength was sapped by malaria.

Frontier doctors were unable to combat infantile diseases. Hard life and lack of medical care kept child mortality at high rate.

The trails West were studded with crosses warning of "cholera," which infested waterholes and brackish streams.

But the frontier had indigenous afflictions beyond the epidemics that ranged in effect from nuisance to agony. Chief among these was the malarial fever known as the ague, which consigned its victims to severe chills and trembling. Few escaped a bout with this disease; in fact, it was so elementary a condition of Western life as to be considered quite normal. "He ain't sick—he only got the ague," was a common remark spoken less in contempt than in familiarity.

Treatment of illness on the frontier largely took the form of homemade remedies. Doctors were scarce and unlikely to be of much help anyway. That the West did not attract the cream of the medical profession was suggested by one homesteader: "The doctor came every day—he purged, he bled, he blistered, he poked—he never cured me." For many patients, whiskey performed yeoman service; it made them dead drunk. And for a people accustomed to hardship, that state came as a cheap if temporary relief.

A frontiersman, lacking doctor's aid, seeks help from an Indian squaw.

The old-time country doctor, dedicated and compassionate, was by today's standards a medical ignoramus.

Doctors

A sickly profession

The country doctor of old—whose image acquires new layers of reverence as medical practice tends toward dispassionate specialization and computerized diagnosis—was actually no more than a venturesome prescriber. Because his diagnosis was based on guesswork his therapy was totally unreliable. Sometimes it cured—often it killed. All things being relative, the comparison with today may seem unfair, but even allowing for the state of the art during the 1860's through the 1890's general practice in the United States was backward, commercial and often fraudulent.

The lack of education and proper licensing exposed the sick to hordes of ignoramuses masquerading as doctors. More a trade than a profession, medicine attracted not the sons of the elite—who preferred law or theology—but mediocrities who saw a chance to get rich quickly. And even this was not enough to satisfy one graduate, who declared, "Hell, if I hadda knowed a feller had to git up every night I would never have started to learn doctoring."

In the latter half of the nineteenth century there were 460 "medical schools," most of them private enterprises run by practitioners who were less concerned with standards than with tuition fees. Students were required to take courses of two 4- to 6-month terms at about $60 a term, and often the second term was a verbatim repetition of the first. These diploma mills, the result of "fusion, fission and spontaneous generation," were manned largely by "professors" who had graduated from similar institutions.

A few of the schools, particularly those connected with universities, had higher standards—although the demand of Dr. Charles Eliot for written examinations was rejected in 1869 by Harvard Medical School with the dean's comment that "a majority of the students cannot write well enough." Dr. Eliot claimed at that time that anyone could walk by Harvard, go in, and "without further question be accepted as a medical student."

Standards began to improve after the opening of Johns Hopkins Medical School in 1893, but on the whole, scientific facilities

Diploma mills cranked out doctors at top speed and at bargain prices.

Doctors were mocked as "inveterate prescribers" feeding medicines of which they knew little into bodies of which they knew less.

remained very primitive compared with those of Edinburgh or Leipzig. Surveying medical schools in the early 1900's, Abraham Flexner was assured by the dean of Salem College (Washington State) that laboratory facilities existed. "I have them upstairs," the dean assured him, "I will bring it to you." And he returned with a small blood pressure instrument.

If diploma mills depressed the standards and quality of general practice, the medical profession as a whole appeared to have abandoned its humanitarian mission in the lust for money. "Crowds of pure tradesmen," is how Dr. L. Connor in 1898 described his colleagues to the American Academy of Medicine. Doctors had little professional prestige; indeed many were considered "crude, coarse and ignorant, contributing to social butchery by keeping the patient ill."

A city doctor's fees in the 1880's —$2 to $3 for office visits; $3 to $6 for house calls—suggest how lucrative a practice could be, and also why so many country doctors, who got 50 cents for house calls, deserted the farm for greener pastures. On an income of $10 a week the average working-class family could hardly afford private medical attention; however, all things considered, this may not have been a disadvantage.

America soon became known as a "bastion of medical humbug," a reputation that prompted Oliver Wendell Holmes to declare: "If the whole materia medica as now used could be sunk to the bottom of the sea, it would be all the better for mankind, and all the worse for the fishes."

Surgery

Surgeons performed with the éclat of battle heroes

General practice was leavened slightly by what might be called "exceptional practice"—sound intuitive diagnoses and treatment by doctors of ability—despite the rudimentary state of medical knowledge. The same held true of surgery—occasional sparks of brilliance on a landscape indistinguishable in character from that of general medical practice.

The textbooks called the period Surgery's Heroic Age. And while it did produce some dashing, imaginative surgeons who "made the abdominal cavity their playground," a question could be raised about who the heroes were —the patients or their doctors?

American surgeons in particular had a reputation for too much dash, a lingering tradition of the Civil War hospitals where amputations were performed in shocking haste—"40 seconds for a leg" —without the benefit of anesthesia. However, in the beginning, even anesthesia proved to be a mixed blessing. With totally unconscious subjects to work on, surgeons became excessively daring and their work actually declined in finesse.

A general indifference to cleanliness—particularly during the "kitchen table" surgery of rural districts—increased the risk of the patient developing septicemia. While there is no evidence that the surgeon smoked during his labors, it is known that he did use instruments that were not always rust-free. His attire typically was street clothes—perhaps a frock coat with sleeves slightly rolled to avoid blood spatterings.

Sutures he kept strung through his lapels or, for greater efficiency, between his teeth.

Although Lister's antiseptic research was well known in the 1870's, it was disregarded by all but a few American surgeons. His carbolic spray to clear the operating room of germs was frowned upon, and even the great Dr. Samuel D. Gross, acknowledged as the "Nestor of American surgeons," questioned the value of the Listerian principle. The death rate in the 1870's of 10 percent for all hospital operations was in large part a consequence of the aftereffects.

There is strong evidence that President Garfield would have survived the bullet wound inflicted by his assassin, Guiteau, in 1881 if Lister's precepts had been followed, but expert doctors called to the President's bedside were said to have probed for the bullet with their fingers and instruments that were far from aseptic. The President died of secondary infection.

Such filthy procedure was typical treatment for accident victims, through whose begrimed limbs, wrote Dr. Stephen Smith, one-time New York City health commissioner, "the surgeon was apt to pass his knife . . . conveying to the deepest part of the wound, matters of untold septic virulence."

Doctors operated in shirt-sleeves or frock coats.

Satire of knife-happy surgeons in one of New York's charity hospitals. Coffins stand ready to receive victims of "Furor Operativus."

Hospitals

"The one nurse slept in the bathroom—the tub was filled with rubbish."

Hospitals, quite clearly, are not an element of the nostalgia for the good old days, and perhaps the absence of curiosity about them suggests a general suspicion that they were, in fact, dreadful places. Even in the criticism of modern hospitals—which often derives from our self-esteem having been bruised by functional coldness—there is not a trace of lament for the past. Nor should there be.

The hospitals, especially in the cities, of the 1860–1900 period were similar to the almshouses, where humanity's castaways languished in appalling squalor. Essentially charitable institutions, they were a last resort for the poor, who did not have home care. The rich and middle classes feared them as pest houses and remained at home when they fell sick, even having operations performed in a bedroom.

Conditions at New York's Bellevue, which has a well-documented history, were typical of the old-fashioned city hospital. Today an institution of medical and administrative excellence, it was founded as a poorhouse near the East River, where "the sluggish tides . . . ebbed and flowed through the sodden soil of its foundation, depositing far more filth than they have removed." Rather than a health-giving resort for the sick, it became a focal point of epidemics, with outbreaks of typhus and typhoid fever in the 1840's taking the lives of half its patients.

A New York society woman, who confessed that in her life she had hardly known hospitals existed, visited Bellevue in 1872, by which time medical services had improved: ". . . the loathsome smell sickened me. The condition of the beds and patients was unspeakable. The one nurse slept in the bathroom and the tub was filled with filthy rubbish."

Ward in Bellevue Hospital, New York, with rats overrunning patients' beds. Authorities admitted "the building is swarming with rats, as many as forty having been killed in a bathroom one evening."

In American hospitals where Florence Nightingale's pioneering work was ignored, the title "nurse" implied no professional training until 1873, when the Bellevue Nursing School was established. Patient care was a common occupation for drunken women, who were permitted to work in a hospital in lieu of serving a prison sentence. Patients well enough to be on their feet were also expected to do ward duty.

Denied basic amenities such as benches, mothers with sick children wait for admission to hospital dispensary.

Such standards of patient care, the total absence of hygiene, and the ward system, in which beds were tightly packed on several floors, made most hospitals veritable deathtraps. Among charity-minded doctors who complained about conditions, a Dr. Dudley in 1899 described New York's Harlem Hospital "as crowded at times as the lowest tenement . . . It is not unusual for us to have from two to six patients sleeping on canvas stretchers on the floor." Outpatients assembled in a shack on the pier. "I have seen hysterical women awaiting care," the doctor reported, "while great ugly wharf rats played in and out of holes and crevices."

Magnifying the inadequacy of the old-time hospital was the fact that the patients usually were very ill, otherwise they would never have consented to being brought there. And by the time many of them were admitted — accident cases were not treated promptly, victims of ailments not caught in time—their chances of recovery had faded. Others deteriorated from hospital-related causes: air so vitiated it was hardly bearable to the healthy, and

Children's hospitals emerging with the new medical branch of pediatrics were often careless in administering vaccines.

surgical methods that were fraught with the hazards of septicemia and gangrene.

The Mayo Clinic and Roosevelt Hospital, N. Y., which in the 1880's had some private rooms at $3 to $5 a day, were exceptions worthy of mention. But these and other fine institutions did little to alter the judgment of the people at large that the hospital was a place to avoid, especially if one valued one's health.

The Mentally Ill

Maltreated and caged like wild beasts

The question of mental illness was bound up in dark suspicion, shame and ignorance. Families hid a demented member as if he were evidence of sin. The poor creatures were kept in attics, in cellars; on Staten Island a lunatic was confined to an outhouse so narrow that "his flexor muscles permanently stiffened." They were totally misunderstood. Dorothy Dix, the staunch crusader for prison and asylum reform, was told: "They don't need any heat—they have no feeling." Those that were unmanageable, violent or without family were committed to the asylum, where to all intents and purposes they no longer belonged to the human race.

In 1887 Nellie Blye, a young reporter for Pulitzer's *New York World* hunting for a scoop, had herself locked up in New York's Blackwell Island Lunatic Asylum, sharing with the inmates vile food, teasing guards and a regimentation fit only for criminals. In her book *Ten Days in a Mad-House* she confessed that the place could easily have driven her to insanity, which no doubt had been the fate of countless inmates who were not demented at all. The most frightful obsession for these unfortunates was the knowledge that they were imprisoned for life in "a human rat trap, easy to get in, impossible to get out."

Thus did Victorian society handle the problem of the mentally ill—confinement instead of treatment, subjugation in place of sympathy. Scant application was made during the 1870's of the new insights into the human

Once trapped in institutions, the insane were confined for life.

mind produced by psychiatry; nor was any attention given to the warning of Dr. S. Weir Mitchell, the great Philadelphia neurologist, that "the alienist is not a jailer." The asylums had some perfunctory medical supervision, but most doctors did not believe insanity curable. Consequently the recovery rate was dismal.

Prior to the enlightened decision to put doctors in charge, asylums were staffed by laymen, indistinguishable from prison guards, who were under the command of "superintendents." Invariably such management was despotic, with the inmates receiving arbitrary punishment for what were considered willful outbursts. The widespread prejudice against the mentally sick (they were regarded as wicked or possessed by some evil) compounded their misery. No matter what their personalities—whether glum, or silent, or spirited; no matter how they behaved, even if they had recovered and were trying desperately to show it—their captors accepted all signs as manifest proof that their charges were indeed crazy. New York's Bloomingdale Hospital (the lunatic asylum attached to New York Hospital) had a reputation for what the *New York Tribune* in 1872 described as the "devilish ignorance, brutality and lewdness" of its management. The *North American Review* observed after an investigation of the state's asylums that the keepers were mostly "shoulder hitters," and that the institutions "would disgrace Turkey with their filth, vermin, contagious disease and food hardly less fatal than starvation."

Life inside had a Dantesque quality as the demented were tormented and the sane driven

mad. An 1878 investigation of the New Jersey State Asylum revealed that in order to detect pretenders, the authorities customarily poured alcohol over epileptic patients and set them on fire. "Treatments" were cold baths and water punishment, which in the depths of winter involved tying a patient to the wall of his cell and dumping buckets of frigid water on him, which caused his head and shoulders to become partially frozen. A frequently applied cure, so called, was "dietary"; in other words, the hunger treatment. A description survives of patients at Ward's Island Asylum in New York City finally getting a meal after a period of applied starvation: ". . . diminutive, dirty bits of meat flanked by a ladleful of oatmeal, dark, nauseating in appearance . . . the women sunk their often dirty fingers into the mush and ate ravenously."

But the most depressing, most harmful aspect of asylum life was the total idleness forced upon

Asylums employed strong male guards to keep the "beast" in place.

the inmates. The word "boredom" cannot fully express the interminable vacancy of their existence as they languished on wooden benches or barren floors, enveloped by the shrieking harangues of their violent co-patients. These unfortunates were cooped up in threes and fours, as in Philadelphia's Old Blockley Hospital, in cells barely 8 by 10 feet. Restraints were necessary, the keepers explained, to prevent rampages, but widespread use of the straitjacket to subdue recalcitrant patients was also an economic measure, being considerably cheaper than hiring extra personnel. Usually these procedures aggravated the conditions they were supposed to mitigate.

Subtleties of human behavior or degrees of illness were lost on asylum management. Whether man or woman, whether a drunk, temporarily disturbed, or even normal but incarcerated through some legal trick, the inmate was damned to anonymity and faceless indifference. *Leslie's Weekly*

in 1882 described a typical madhouse as presenting "the most soul-sickening sights, if not the most harrowing ... the wild shrieks, the babel of confused sounds, the vagrant eyes, the disheveled hair."

Doctors of the period remarked on the high incidence of insanity in America. In his article, "Despotism in Lunatic Asylums," Dr. D. B. Eaton noted that insanity "had become more frequent and more fatal"—at a ratio of increase far exceeding that of the population. And the causes of this increase were, according to Dr. George Beard's classic treatise *American Nervousness,* the country's rapid growth, the displacement of people by the movement West, and the overcrowding of the cities.

But whatever the causes, the effects on asylum facilities were devastating. Although many new state hospitals were built in the 1890's, critics asserted that more attention was paid to structural elegance than to improving conditions for the inmates.

Left to themselves the inmates' condition worsened. Normal people, confined through trickery, were apt to go mad.

Feeding time, Old Blockley Hospital, Philadelphia. Starved inmates grabbed meager meals with their fingers.

The padded cell
was the safest method
of sequestering the
deranged and a means
of avoiding costly
custodial care.

The excuse for
the strait jacket
was that it kept
the insane from
harming themselves.

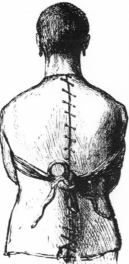

"I have seen
insane women naked
and helpless sitting
in empty dungeons."

The violence of the insane was considered willful
insubordination to be brutally punished.

Insane woman confined to "crib" in New York State institution, 1882.

Drug Addiction

An apocalypse of horror

End of the morphine addict.

That essentially American problem, drug addiction, has a longer history than most of us may suspect. Opium use, which had become a national habit as early as 1840, found its devotees in all classes and regions. An expert's estimate put the number of drug addicts at 100,000 in 1868, a year that witnessed a sixfold increase over 1840 in the importation of opium (from 24,000 to 146,000 pounds.)

An Ohio doctor claimed that in his town addicts outnumbered alcoholics, and Lafcadio Hearn described the drug scene in Cincinnati (1871): "Walk along the streets any day and you will meet opium slaves by the score. . . . They are slaves, abject slaves

suffering exquisite torture. Once in the fetters of opium and morphia, they are, with few exceptions, fettered for life." A clergyman of the same city, unable to face his congregation without the support of opium, committed suicide shortly before his service.

A mixture of ignorance, unhappiness and susceptibility to quick palliatives was responsible for the growing addiction to opium, which, in Hearn's words, was "settling down upon America and gorging its victims." Writers and artists—the intellectual class —were heavy users; William James experimented with drugs, which gave him "the most glorious vision of color and jeweled splendor, unknown to the natural world." But he was philosophical enough to warn that the drugs

The alarming rise in drug addiction brought forth spurious offers to cure it.

The Chinese were accused of using opium dens to practice white slavery.

that bring "man from the chilled periphery of things to the radiant core [are] in their totality . . . a degrading poison."

Jane Addams describes a group of vagrant Chicago youngsters huddled in an abandoned building to seek relief from their wretched life in the euphoria of drugs: "They stole from their parents, pawned their clothes and shoes, did any desperate thing to get 'the dope,' as they called it." The drugstores sold opium openly then, in pill form or as laudanum by the bucket, in addition to all kinds of habit-forming potions masquerading as cures. But the comfort these various nostrums provided was temporary at best, and often fatal.

Thousands of ex-soldiers were addicts, having acquired the habit as battlefield casualties of the Civil War who had been given laudanum to alleviate their agonies. And for even the most innocent people the danger of addiction was ominously present in the patent medicines that were popular and readily available. Many of these had a base of 30 to 40 percent alcohol—apart from their opiate content—and were blamed for the high rate of drunkenness in America. A sip of Peruna had as much of a kick as a martini, and it was believed that more alcohol was inbibed via patent medicine than in the form of bottled liquor.

Infants, too, were exposed to the danger of drugs. No mother of the 1880's would be caught without Winslow's Baby Syrup or Kopp's Baby Friend, which was liberally spiked with morphine. Both medicines could indeed put the child to sleep, but at the risk of addiction for life.

More from ignorance than greed, doctors abetted, and often created, the sinister craving by their careless prescribing of opiates, which occupied about 75 percent of their medical bags. Drugging was almost the only kind of relief they could provide the sick, who in most cases would have been better served if nature had been allowed to take its course.

The Narcotics Drug Act of 1909 demonstrated the federal government's concern, but the use of drugs remained very high, reaching in pre-World War I days, for opium alone, a per capita intake eighteen times higher than that of Germany. The drug addiction of today—a most painful reflection on American society—had its origin in the good old days.

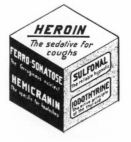

The pharmaceutical firm of Bayer gave the world aspirin; it also developed heroin and marketed it as a cough medicine (1898).

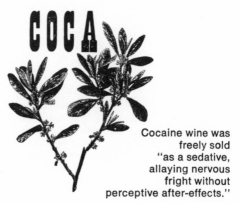

Cocaine wine was freely sold "as a sedative, allaying nervous fright without perceptive after-effects."

Teachers drilled facts and moral precepts into young minds.
Recitation was stressed as training for future orators.
The McGuffey Reader, America's educational best seller,
was intended to train the voice rather than the mind.

9 Education

CRITICISM of the public school system — America's most jealously treasured institution — usually takes the form of nostalgia for its "Golden Age," the days of the Little Red Schoolhouse. Here, it is believed, was the wellspring of the nation's greatness, where the three R's were taught in an atmosphere of patriotism and simple virtue, where individualism was sanctified, the warts of alien culture were ground away and, finally, the American character was shaped.

In a time of widespread educational hysteria it is a vision hard to resist; however, it is not an accurate one. The little schoolhouse was the dispensary of only limited information — much of it questionable — that was force-fed to pupils. Thinking was discouraged in favor of memorizing prepackaged "noble" thoughts, and the three R's were imparted with a painful repetition associated more with the training of a dog. Good spelling was a major goal — more even than word meaning — and the classroom resounded like a parade ground to the monotonous cadence of vowels and consonants. (The spelling bee, an American phenomenon that confuses the rapid emission of facts with true knowledge, survives in our quiz programs.)

Recalling his own school days during the 1880's, Alvin Johnson, the great educator, said, "We expected to learn nothing in school and we were not disappointed."

Country Teacher

A man who had failed at everything bought himself a birch rod and became a teacher.

Rural schools were handicapped not only by size—one room for all ages—but by the quality of instruction they dispensed. Teaching was an occupation of minimal prestige, with low pay, low standards and a high turnover rate. It was said that anybody could be a teacher, and while no doubt some were fine, dedicated individuals, most proved shiftless and unimaginative—products of the very system they perpetuated.

Because children supplied essential farm labor, the school year lasted barely twelve weeks, from Thanksgiving through early spring. It was hardly enough time for learning, or to encourage a teacher who genuinely sought results. And the salaries—in 1888–89 an average of $42.43 a month for men and $38.14 for women, grudgingly relinquished from frugal budgets—attracted mostly young men in transit to a profession or women who declared themselves schoolmarms to get away from a suffocating home life. Sometimes the teacher was a girl younger than several of her pupils, and almost as ignorant.

Teachers were compensated for their low pay by being allowed to alternate free board and lodgings with various families. But many could not endure the accompanying scrutiny given their private lives and quit in disgust after a term or two, leaving the curriculum in chaos. Clarence Darrow recalls: "We seldom had the same teacher for two terms of school, and we always wondered whether the new one would be worse or better than the old."

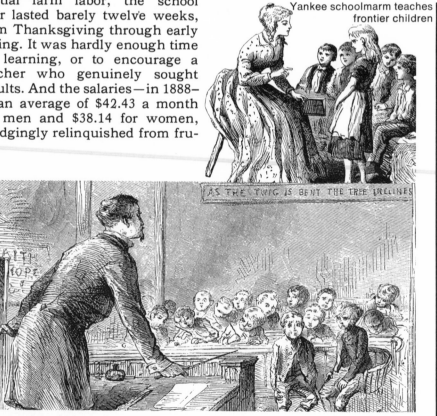

Yankee schoolmarm teaches frontier children

AS THE TWIG IS BENT THE TREE INCLINES

Laying down the law: no deviation from the teaching routine was tolerated. Students had to memorize lessons whether they understood them or not.

Corporal Punishment

"Lickin' and larnin' goes together, No lickin', no larnin'"

The little red schoolhouse didn't always look as trim as we imagine. Often it was a dilapidated structure, painted with red ocher, the cheapest paint available.

The foregoing dogma was basic to the educational philosophy of the old days. Lessons were regarded as a commodity to be pressed into reluctant vessels—the pupils—and a birch rod or hickory stick was used to accomplish this end. Legally *in loco parentis,* teachers relied upon it more heavily to enforce discipline, their devotion to scholarship often measured by the number of backsides they had reddened.

Humanitarians, a tiny minority, thought otherwise, among them a former schoolmaster named Walt Whitman, who complained of the "military discipline" of the schools. "The flogging plan is the most wretched item yet of school-keeping," he thundered. "What nobleness can reside in a man who catches boys by the collar, and cuffs their ears?"

But such criticism posed no threat to corporal punishment, which was extensively hailed as a healthy and indispensable practice. (One inveterate disciplinarian referred to his weapon as "my board of education.") And concomitant with this belief went an austere mistrust of improvements to the physical plant because they were a "luxury." A Washington Territory schoolmarm's plea for the installation of toilets was turned down by the school board, which advised her that "there were plenty of trees in the yard to get behind." Even her suggestion to replace the single well dipper with more hygienic individual cups was denied as being "undemocratic."

Caught napping.

Rule of the ferule.

Discipline?

Pandemonium in the classroom

The indisputable reality of classroom disorder presented a valid case against appeals for an end to birching. The Little Red Schoolhouse was not a stable of docile lambs; many of the children were downright brats—hostile, ungovernable and prone to violence. In addition, the assembly in one room of pupils ranging in age from five to sixteen, with some strays even in their twenties, was an invitation to trouble.

Under these circumstances the teacher was more warder than instructor, his routine more physical than intellectual. Some school boards in selecting a new teacher made it a rule to pick a strong fellow—especially on the frontier, where, according to Hamlin Garland, "baseness and vulgarity" prevailed among the older boys. Biting, eye-gouging and slug and scuffle matches were favorite sports, but boys saved their most barbaric excesses for strangers.

"Let a boy from one town visit another and he was fortunate if he escaped with his life. The intervillage feuds made it incumbent upon the boys of one town to stone, beat, thrash such a casual visitor." Faced with such ruffians, many teachers did not last a week, some not even a day; "In Flat Crick district," says Edward Eggleston, "the boys have driven off the last two schoolmasters and licked the one afore them." Villagers and their school boards took macabre delight in the encounter between a new teacher and the "boys," some of whom were 175-pound six-footers. For schoolmarms such confrontations were an ordeal even in the East. Describing her first day at a New England District school, Mary Ellen Chase recalls: "I stormed up and down . . . This pathetic pretense of courage, aided by the mad flourishing of my razor

The little red schoolhouse was not a stable of docile lambs. Young children were unruly, older ones rough and base.

THE VILLAGE SCHOOL

strop, brought forth . . . the expression of respectful fear on the faces of the young giants."

However, while Miss Chase's pantomime succeeded in cowing heavyweights who were old enough to go to sea, other schoolmistresses encountered continual disciplinary problems. One of these, a Miss Barstow, taught public school in Canton, Mass. On October 8, 1870, the young woman, said to be in feeble health, punished four boys for unruly conduct by shutting them in the school building after class was out. Finally, when she released them, Miss Barstow is said to have given the boys "a slight reprimand." Their response was immediate; they stoned her to death.

Miss Etta A. Barstow,
a young schoolteacher,
stoned to death
by her pupils
in Canton, Massachusetts,
October 8, 1870.

Miss Barstow on the stoop of her home where she was found close to death.

Negro Education

Compulsory ignorance

As early as 1836 Prudence Crandall's school for black children was destroyed in Canton, Connecticut.

Of the four million slaves freed after the Civil War, only one in ten could read and write. Throughout the first half of the century, slaveholders had been assiduous in keeping them ignorant; knowledge, they feared, would breed insurrection. Some states made teaching a Black child a crime, and Governor James Kimball Vardaman of Mississippi, a wild Negrophobe, declared that any money spent on Black education was "a robbery of the white man."

The shame and hypocrisy of these sanctions were condemned by Northern abolitionists, who diagnosed the black man's trouble: "We deliberately withhold from him the humanizing and softening influences of education—and then we reproach him that he is not thrifty, not enlightened, not virtuous. . . . Doing our best to make him a bad citizen, we reproach him for not being a good one." But their high hopes, following the Civil War, of providing the freedman's children with an elementary education went largely unfulfilled. State constitutions, amended to give Blacks separate but equal education, were blithely ignored. Promised budgetary funds were simply never paid, and school facilities remained totally unequal.

W. E. B. DuBois, the educator, has left an account of the Black school: ". . . a loghut where Colonel Wheeler used to shelter his corn . . . chinks between the logs served as windows . . . My chair borrowed from the landlady had to be returned every night." There were no desks, and crude backless planks served as seats, which "had the one virtue of making napping dangerous."

Black scholars lacking classrooms learned their lessons on the street.

City Schools

"Our public schools going to the dogs"

In 1890, only 20 percent of all Negro children received any education at all, and their lifetime schooling averaged 100 days.

In reviewing the pitiful conditions of early Black schools there is a temptation to assume the opposite about white public schools. But such assumptions would not be entirely accurate. City schools were badly neglected as political bosses ransacked educational funds. And they did this with impunity, since the board of education was appointed by aldermen who were appointed by the mayor, who was controlled by the bosses.

In this game of spending "less public money on education and more on themselves," Tweed of New York was, of course, the champion. Not only did he mulct funds assessed for new school buildings, but he connived to have all city schoolbooks scrapped in order to profit from the sale of new books produced by Tweed-controlled printing plants. Nor was this handicap to education limited to New York City. St. Louis, Philadelphia and Chicago, among others, had their own educational "Tweed days."

Consequently city schools were overcrowded and underventilated, compounding the difficulty of teaching youngsters of various ethnic backgrounds. Many teachers confessed that the best they could do was to "maintain order," and the New York commissioner of education frankly admitted in 1871 that "thousands of children leave school without being able to read and write."

Catholics insisted on parochial schools. They would lead to "American Popery," Protestants feared. Children were caught up in this conflict.

SECTARIAN BITTERNESS.

Dismal Classrooms

"In New York children are forced to attend schools which in foulness could put to shame a refuse vault."

The American compulsion to spend unlimited sums on ultramodern school buildings may contain a hint of delusion, but it can be appreciated more readily when examined against the schools of the past. To begin with, there were not sufficient buildings, and those that did exist were poorly constructed and maintained, filthy, and invariably overcrowded—the last being the most dangerous of their evils. Schools built for 1000 pupils had twice that number jammed into their classrooms. A survey of Brooklyn schools in 1893 listed 18 classes with 90 to 100 students; one class had 158. Desks were insufficient and badly made; often three children shared a desk built for two.

A visitor to Cincinnati in the same year found one schoolroom where "the furniture was so closely packed that the children were literally obliged to squeeze their little bodies in between the desks ... scarcely room enough ... to expand their lungs, much less to move their limbs about freely." To one observer, the city school, where the children's "chests were sunken, their shoulders rounded," was a factory of hunchbacks. And a New York slum school (perched over a live chicken market), lacking chairs and benches, had its students study on their knees.

New York City schools were encumbered by their location, which precluded access to adequate lighting or ventilation. Crammed into narrow streets and overshadowed by taller buildings or an adjacent elevated railroad, the schoolrooms frequently were lighted by only a single jet whose flickering spread an "atmosphere of melancholy and gloom, its yellow flame blazing into the teacher's eye, leaving the scholars insufficient light to read their books."

Air quality proved as deficient as the lighting. A Massachusetts law required 1800 cubic feet of fresh air per hour per child; in New York students got closer to 70 cubic feet. "The air . . . became so vitiated, foul and unhealthy that teachers were compelled to suspend the studies."

A risk of infectious disease was present in the classrooms in the absence of bodily cleanliness, par-

Schools jostled factories and slaughterhouses. Children had no playground; nor could they play on the street, which was filled with roaming cattle.

DISEASE AND DEATH

The Public Schools Breed Cripples
and Deformities.

SQUALOR AND FILTH THE RULE

The Children Losing Their Eyesight
and Becoming Humpbacked---Curv-
ature of the Spine the Prevalent Dis-
ease---That Beneficent Board of Education and its Splendid Work.

Students became listless because of "germ-laden atmosphere . . . in places wretched for the body . . . dwarfing for the mind."

ticularly among immigrant children, who descended on the schools like a great army of the unwashed. "The teachers . . . found themselves giving hundreds of baths each week," and one small student answered his teacher's criticism of his appearance with, "Don't never wash—ketch cold."

One of the most serious handicaps to systematic instruction, at least in New York City, was noise. "I have seen one teacher made voiceless and many made hoarse by the constant shouting necessitated by sounds from adjoining buildings and the maddening bang and crash of hammers." These external noises, including the omnipresent racket of the El, were supplemented by the self-generated din and babble of the classrooms.

Scavenger forages at entrance to New York slum school. Jacob Riis photo.

Boarded-up, dilapidated room serves as school for New York ghetto boys.

Effluvia of playrooms, often built over sewer system, dazed even school inspectors.

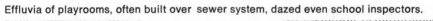

Teaching Methods

". . . Each child is treated as if he possessed no individuality, no soul."

Dr. J. M. Rice, a pediatrician turned educator, found little difference among primary schools in thirty-six cities. Education had been devalued to a factory-style routine in which the pupils were regarded as exactly similar and therefore could be drilled with mechanical efficiency. In a St. Louis school he reported children lined up stiffly, "silent and motionless," during recitation, their toes aligned along the edge of a floorboard. All spontaneity had been suppressed in favor of a queer obsession with symmetry: "How can you learn anything with your knees and toes out of order?" a teacher demanded.

Darrow recalled that beyond "Yes, ma'am" or "No, ma'am" children were prohibited from speaking. "It was assumed that what we had to say was of no account." The pupil was totally subjugated by the teacher, who was advised. "Do what you like with the child . . . immobilize him, automatize him, but save the minutes."

Rice noticed a very literal interpretation of this advice in New York City classrooms, where students were prohibited from even moving their heads. "Why should they look behind when the teacher is in front of them?" he was asked. The humorless, bloodless approach to teaching so typical of the period. is captured in his description of a Chicago pedagogue, who "never smiled or offered the slightest encouragement . . . she sat in a chair as sober as a judge trying a criminal case . . . most of her students while speaking were trembling from head to foot."

Naturally, neither truancy nor dropping out was discouraged by such a system. Although by the 1870's compulsory education was the law in most states, poorer families—particularly immigrants—preferred to have their children at work than at school; often the pay scale made it a matter of survival. In New York's blighted Five Points area, only 9 children out of 600 attended school in 1870.

For the poor who did attend school, there was an added handicap to the stultifying method of instruction—hunger. Figures for New York, Philadelphia, Buffalo and Chicago in 1905 showed that of 40,746 schoolchildren 34 percent left home either without breakfast or after having had a totally inadequate one of unwholesome bread and tea. No wonder these students were listless and the despair of the teachers who realized that "You cannot educate a hungry child." In 1904 Dr. W. H. Maxwell, the head of the Board of Education of New York, said that the number of U.S. schoolchildren unable to learn as a result of hunger was in the hundreds of thousands.

The alternative for some poor children was to work during the day and attend night school, where it was felt they could prepare better for work in a factory. In any event, the working class regarded elementary education as impractical because it offered subjects that had no application to the new industrial order.

Pictures on opposite page, Museum of the City of New York.

Children sat tightly packed, following the lessons like robots. Strict regimentation would make the next generation of New Yorkers nearsighted, deaf and hysterical, it was said.

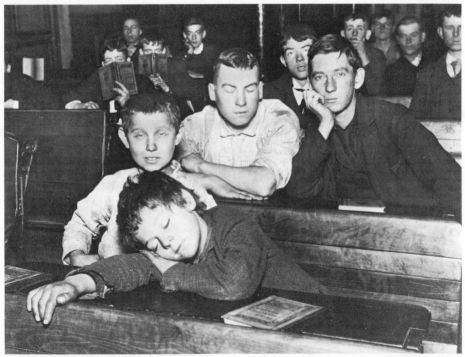

Boys compelled to work all day to help support the family came to night school exhausted, and often hungry. Reformers warned "You cannot teach a hungry child—nor a tired one."

Teachers

"... subsist on a pittance; they must pinch and save until life is not worth living."

The grade school was born of necessity in the 1870's. The one-room building had become totally inadequate for city populations, and the idea of separate and progressive grades was intelligent and practical. It would have been an ideal system if the teaching had been adequate. But it wasn't.

Before 1900, teaching was not a bona fide profession. Teachers' institutes gave informal lectures, graduating anyone who served a brief apprenticeship, and in regular "normal schools," which had a slightly higher standing, only 20 percent of students in 1890 had high school diplomas. Chicago's requirements were similarly casual; no diploma was required, and any young man or woman could become a teacher if they accompanied an incumbent on his rounds as part of a "cadet program."

But even teachers of natural ability became quickly demoralized by the low pay, lack of promotion, and graft-ridden appointment system, and their performance reflected it. Their salaries, subject to the whims of the school board, often went down when the budget was cut. Favoritism, too, was general, and a teacher with good connections could get double the salary of a colleague who had none. Women teachers suffered greatly as a result of the chafing sex discrimination of the period—for the same work they got less than half a male teacher's salary. After five years' service in New York City schools they could expect a raise of $40 a year—that is, if they had not married or "engaged in other unseemly conduct," which invariably meant dismissal.

Despite the poor wages, teaching jobs belonged to the patronage concessions held by politicians. During the Tweed era, a time of

Janitors, political appointees, had safe and well-paid jobs.

First step in "economy drives" was to cut teachers' salaries.

extensive pioneering in government corruption, jobs were actually auctioned. Merit, of course, counted for nothing. Philadelphia's school boards were considered even more corrupt than New York's, having as they did enormous shakedown charges: $120 for a teaching job; $175 for a transfer between schools.

The word "education" means to draw out: to develop the sentient and intellectual qualities that are inborn. But what passed for education in the 1890's, as the elementary grade school became fully developed, had only a remote connection with its original concept.

"Making grades" was the only goal, and the excessively heavy curricula meant endless cramming for students, without any time left to contemplate what it was they were learning. A young girl of the 1880's described her anxiety after a day's drilling, her whole time having been taken up with reviews while she "trembled every minute for fear I shall forget some date of history or rule in algebra . . . When I finally sit down to dinner my head feels fit to burst."

Often poorly educated themselves, the teachers stuck rigidly to the manual prescribed by the board. Many were interested in neither the pupils nor their jobs and took the easy way out by becoming little more than "drillmasters" and "recitation hearers."

Teachers crammed facts into the student
to ensure his promotion from grade to grade.

Accidents faced travelers at every turn.
Trains collided, bridges collapsed,
ferry and riverboats exploded.

10 Travel

In a world where jet travel is commonplace for the common man, it is difficult to comprehend that less than a century ago the horizon for most people was limited to the spot where fate had deposited them. For the affluent, traveling via steam packet, Pullman train or stagecoach was often a costly ordeal where consideration of human comfort and safety was at best an afterthought. The most fearful means of transportation was also the most widely used — the railroad.

Train wrecks due to broken trestles, poor track, exploding boilers, faulty signals, and careless engineers and switchmen were a daily occurrence, producing an accident rate in the United States five times that of England. In 1890 railroad-connected accidents caused 10,000 deaths and 80,000 serious injuries. And while the primitive technology had built-in dangers, railroad management was the real villain, prompting George T. Strong to diarize: "We shall never travel safely till some pious, wealthy, and much beloved railroad director has been hanged for murder. . . ."

Ocean travel of the period was both magnificent and squalid. The great liners, called "floating hotels," competed for the rich with palatial appointments — in themselves no guarantee for safe arrival. Steerage passengers were out of sight, penned away belowdecks in their floating slums.

Steerage

A traumatic trip led to the Promised Land

Aboard ship, "steerage" refers to the underdeck compartments near the rudder—a region without light or ventilation. And that is where more than 90 percent of the 10,339,000 emigrants en route to America between 1870 and 1895 were quartered. Travel on the great liners of the period—considered "the only way to go" by the rich—had steerage as its counterpart, where the emigrants were treated like cattle. "Neither officers nor men consider them worthy of the least respect."

These underprivileged passengers had to prepare their own meals; normally two galleys five by four feet were the only cooking facilities provided for several hundred persons. Most slept on the floor—lucky if they could get some straw, privileged if they could occupy a bunk consisting of five-foot planks in tiers of four. Robert Louis Stevenson wrote of the impossibility of keeping

Immigrant ships—"floating coffins."

the steerage or its inhabitants clean. To him it was a "dim inferno, with the ship rattling and rolling intermixed with the coughing and retching of the sick and the frightened sob of children." Most of the vessels were dilapidated and slow—the *James Foster* in 1869 took ten weeks from Liverpool to New York—and were known as fever ships or floating coffins. Hungry, huddled together in overcrowded spaces, the emigrants weakened as the voyage progressed.

Facing starvation, immigrants were gripped by fear. Some went mad.

Upper-class comfort.

Emigrant accommodations.

During storms when hatches had to be closed, steerage passengers rushed on deck to avoid suffocation—and risked being swept overboard.

The Emigrant Train

A Noah's Ark on wheels

The Gilded Age was embodied in the private railroad car—a baroque equipage of millionaires that today may be found in museums. But there is little trace of the carriages in which the masses were transported, only the memories of those who rode them.

To Robert Louis Stevenson, the emigrant train on which he traveled West in 1879 resembled a series of long wooden boxes— a "Noah's Ark on wheels." Wooden benches were their only furniture, "far too short for anyone but a child," and the atmosphere was stagnant with the smells of food and tobacco. Families and single men and women shared these rolling slums, cooking, washing perfunctorily, and at night sleeping on wooden boards stretched across the benches. The rate for these "beds," which included three straw- (and bug-) filled cushions, was $2.50.

"Switched off." Immigrants had to evacuate their car to make room for urgent cattle shipments.

Except for rare acts of kindness, the poor emigrants met nothing but rudeness from train functionaries, who even refused to answer their anxious inquiries. "Civility is the main comfort you miss," Stevenson remarked. "Equality, though very largely conceived in America, does not extend so low down as the emigrant."

Dumped on railroad siding at the end of their trip, emigrants were often left in a state of confusion, if not despair.

Immigrants were shipped West in worn-out, filthy boxcars
attached to freight or cattle trains.

Ordeals Of Railroading

Crowded stations—baggage smashers—demonic stoves

New York railway stations, filled with crowds to escape summer heat, attracted city's young pickpockets.

The railroads performed two historical functions: They united the nation and mistreated its citizenry. Even Lucius Beebe, that great romancer of the iron horse and its trail of cinders, confessed: "The American public rode to dusty destinies in regimented discomfort."

Their discomfort began at the station, which has also been eulogized by romantics as a charming social center. In fact it was a convocation of loafers and spittoons, usually in the charge of a stationmaster who treated both passengers and baggage with undisguised contempt. Late arrivals and departures were aggravated by the absence of the "check system" for baggage, which had to be identified and retrieved by the passengers themselves. Often this led to lengthy arguments and the smashing of trunks and

Cars were heated by open iron stoves which often overturned, causing a fire when the train had an accident.

suitcases on the platform. The country station in particular depressed foreigners, who saw in it "unqualified ugliness and chilling desolation." Despite the lore attached to the conductor's chronometer, train schedules of the period might as well have been calibrated by sundial or calendar—especially on small trunk lines in winter. Connections were more miss than hit, partly because of competing railroads. A traveler from Woodstock, Vt., in 1888 took two days to get to New York City; the response to his inquiry about when a certain train would leave was a laconic "Sometime." R. L. Dufus reminisces that in the same part of New England the train took "two and a half hours to carry us from Williamstown, Vt., to Waterbury, Vt., a distance of 24 miles . . . a jet plane could cover this in two minutes."

The middle class made up the bulk of passenger traffic, and the conditions they endured were closer to the emigrant carriages than to the private railroad car. The old wood-burning locomotives belched cinders that pattered overhead like a hailstorm, and their smoke and steam engulfed the train until, at journey's end, the traveler found himself "begrimed like a man who has worked all day in a blacksmith's . . ."

The alternative was to close the windows and suffer the stenches of whiskey, tobacco and closely packed bodies, stenches which remained imprisoned in the cars despite ceiling grills installed to ventilate them. Frequently those who elected for ashes and cinder dust over suffocation were unable to budge the windows—then, as now, a mystery of design. Incessant noise was an added handicap that drowned all but the loudest voices.

Unlike European trains, which offered small compartments to reduce noise and bodily discomfort, American railroads in democratic fashion herded sixty to seventy passengers into each long car. The backs of the seats were too low to act as headrests, and if a passenger managed to nap in spite of the odds against him he was soon awakened by the "trainboy," a peddler of books, candy and sundry goods whose visitations were constant and disruptive. Mark Twain on his way West was badgered by what he called their "malignant outrages." He also noted that his fellow passengers looked "fearfully unhappy . . . doubled up in uncomfortable attitudes, on short seats in the dim funereal light . . . like so many corpses who had died of care and weariness."

Southern railroads were notoriously dirty but meticulous in enforcing Jim Crow law.

Pullman Cars

Infernal dormitories

Pullman's self-contained sleeping car, introduced in the late 1860's, was regarded as a milestone in transportation luxury. And so it may have appeared to

Baggage cars were called "arenas of destruction." Trunks were dumped on platform by expert "baggage-smasher."

Getting into one's bed was an acrobatic feat.

"wooden-board" veterans, but to many others it fell short of being a pleasurable experience. "You only can get dressed in them if you know how to dress under a sofa."

Sleep was made difficult by the bad air trapped behind heavy curtains, the jolting of the train, and the overall cacophony of snores and crying babies.

Arnold Bennett confessed to never having imagined "anything as appalling as the confined, stifling, malodorous promiscuity of the American sleeping car."

Railroad food: scrambling and trampling for the indigestible

The Pullman dining car had critics too; Walter Besant, the English novelist, called its fare "a greasy pretense." For reasons of both economy and space the great majority of passengers never set foot inside the dining car; instead they gobbled at lunchrooms located along the line.

These stopovers for meals were cruelly brief—five to ten minutes —and travelers were forced to develop hoglike eating habits.

"Scrambling and trampling for the indigestible."

"Half done with his meal, the traveler heard the engine's whistle start a wrathful summons, heard the conductor and the brakemen cry, 'All aboard!' saw his fellow-passengers break for the door, trampling waitresses, tossing coins, dashing for the cars in terror of being left."

Commuters

"Most long-suffering and patient of men"

Perhaps it is with the commuters of the 1880's that we today find the closest spiritual link, for they, too, had complaints that were perennial. The railroads, as might be guessed, were the prime offenders. They had created the suburbs by running track to outlying hamlets, producing a daily bonanza of captive passengers to whom they blithely gave dismal service.

The northern suburbs in Westchester and Fairfield counties were brought into being by Vanderbilt's Hudson River Railroad and the New Haven just as the Old Colony Railroad had made Quincy, Mass., Boston's bedroom community. But insufficient train service and frequent breakdowns, along with extortionate fares, kept commuters in a state of perpetual outrage. The worst record belonged to the Long Island, the Pennsylvania Railroad's unlucky stepchild.

P. T. Barnum, one of the earliest promoters of suburbia and a shrewd developer of Fairfield County, Conn., was a prominent victim of the Vanderbilt-controlled Harlem Division, which he was forced to rely on to get to New York. Not wanting to be a "sucker," he denounced the commuter line for its continual attempts to raise the price of tickets (usually issued for a full year and unlimited rides—New York to White Plains cost $100).

Today's commuter—freezing on the platform in winter, sweltering in summer, running for trains, his blood pressure soaring when one of them gets stuck— would have found kindred souls in the commuters of the 1880's, whom William Dean Howells described as "suburbanly bundled men, that hurry their work all day to catch the evening train out, hurrying their dreams all night to catch the morning train in."

"Another Long Island Railroad outrage." Drenched commuters wait for Brooklyn train at Woodhaven Tower.

Ferries during the rush hour were overloaded with passengers and horse-drawn carriages that competed for room in open scambles.

Harbor Accidents

Fire on the water

After the opening of the Brooklyn Bridge in 1883, commuters from King's County and Long Island were relieved of their dependency on the East River ferries. But New Jerseyans had to wait for their hour of liberation (in a way, they are still waiting). The Hudson River ferries of the eighties carried horse traffic as well as commuters, and because their schedules were erratic, enormous melees broke out at docking. In the rush to be first on or off, many commuters would leap before the vessel actually touched, and not a few were drowned or crushed to death between bow and wharf. When in winter the river froze, ferry service stopped.

River collisions in fog were a grave danger during those pre-radar days; ferry pilots were tense—"passengers strive with eager eyes to pierce the mist. . . . From either side the clangor of ferry bells comes floating . . . and all around steamers are shrieking their shrill signals."

The apprehension was well justified, for not all ferry commuters made it ashore safely. New York Harbor was the scene of frequent tragedy. On July 11, 1871, the ferry *Westfield* exploded with such fury that 104 passengers were literally blown to pieces. Later it was disclosed that her boiler had corroded to such a degree "a knife blade could cut through its metal." Reports such as this caused New Yorkers to fear all through these years "that a terrible accident on a riverboat is imminent at all times."

The boilers of these vessels— subject to no rigorous design or

Boiler Inspection: "They seem to have done all they could in the way of patching . . . We will give them another certificate . . . surely it will last . . . till it blows up."

maintenance codes—were as lethal as bombs, and the danger to life was magnified by the malfunction of on-board safety equipment, or indeed its absence. An explosion blew up the Long Island Sound steamer *Seewanhaka* on June 28, 1880, causing sixty-two deaths. And twenty-four years later, in 1904, continuing disregard for public safety led to a holocaust on board the river liner *General Slocum*. On a day cruise up the East River with 1350 passengers—mostly women and children—the *General Slocum* caught fire at 83rd Street, and by the time it reached 110th Street it was a funeral pyre. Children "rushed blazing like torches to their mothers." Many jumped overboard, clothes aflame. All 400 children, members of St. Mark's German Lutheran Church, perished; only 170 of all passengers survived.

Even the old Mississippi "salon steamer" riverboats were hazardous, notwithstanding their outward magnificence that conjures up visions of "passengers cruising up the river sipping mint julep beneath gently whooshing fans." In reality they were less glamorous—crowded to capacity, bustling with gambling sharks and ruffians and pervaded by the compound aroma of food, cattle excrement and decaying straw. And explosions, fires and collisions were the order of the day.

Travel in the old days, by rail or steamship, was less remarkable for speed than for death through negligence. In man-made disasters caused by flimsy construction, the period holds an unenviable record.

Steamer catastrophe on Long Island Sound. The *Narrangansett*, after her collision with the *Stonington*.

Father working away in the counting house is
vainly implored by his daughter to join a family outing
"Make more money" was the American imperative.
Yet a better living rarely meant a better life.

11 Leisure

LEISURE HAS BECOME a primary component of American life — coequal with the necessities and not merely a random gratuity of hard work. But less than a hundred years ago it was not even an expectation; in fact, the meaning of leisure was not clearly understood. For the working masses, vacations did not exist. For those above subsistence level, ideology got in the way, their imperative of success producing a tireless rhythm of life where relaxation was tantamount to laziness, a cardinal sin in the land of sweat and gold. As Thomas Low Nichols observed: "In no country is there so much toilsome, unremitting labor — in none so little of recreation and enjoyment of life."

Because leisure did not belong in the American scheme of things, facilities for it were meager. And what did exist tended to appeal to rough and vulgar tastes. Gambling was widespread and crooked, sports unregulated and cruel; sportsmanship as we practice it today was not understood.

Certain cultural pursuits, such as theater and music, were accessible to middle-class city dwellers, but their single-minded devotion to making money left little time for renewal "in the byways of life." Charles Dudley Warner, who with Mark Twain wrote *The Gilded Age,* found Americans unfit for leisure because they applied to it "a form of serious energy used to build a railroad."

Gambling

America's oldest diversion deteriorated into a vice

In the turn of a card or the roll of a dice for all or nothing, there was a kind of daring that touched the American spirit. "The lust for work is matched . . . by the lust to gamble." The affluent risked thousands in comfort; the poor risked bread money on gaming tables in slum taverns.

The gambling fever produced two opposing species. First were the predatory card sharps and confidence men who understood human weakness and how to exploit it; second were the masses, eternally gullible to the lure of something for nothing. Throughout the nation these adversaries met—in lotteries, over tables, at racetracks, in casinos, cockpits— and the result was nearly always the same. The suckers lost.

In 1870, New York had an estimated 2500 illegal gambling houses, which produced, as they did elsewhere, crime and degeneracy. And while these are hardly the by-products one would expect of a leisure activity, it should be remembered that vice can become a pastime for people who had little alternative resource.

"A sucker has no more chance against those fellows than a snowball has on a red hot stove."

Animal baiting was the favored leisure-time activity of New York's rougher element. In Kit Burns' Sportsmen's Hall on Water Street, huge gray rats from the waterfront that had been starved for days were set against each other with heavy betting on prospective survivors.

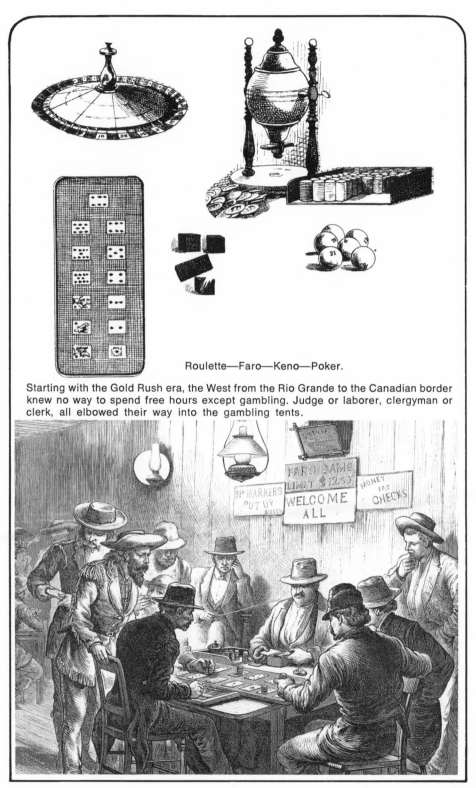

Roulette—Faro—Keno—Poker.

Starting with the Gold Rush era, the West from the Rio Grande to the Canadian border knew no way to spend free hours except gambling. Judge or laborer, clergyman or clerk, all elbowed their way into the gambling tents.

Hunting

A rampage of senseless killing

Although hunting as a leisure activity did not have the widespread following it does today, the devastation of wildlife was far greater. Hunters engaged in outright butchery, often using great flocks of birds for mere target practice. Mallard, duck and pheasant were killed by the thousands in orgies of shooting, and there were countless incidents of hunters never bothering to count their bag, but leaving hundreds of dead birds to rot on the ground.

Sports hunters belonged largely to the middle and upper classes, as ordinary citizens had neither the time nor the money to travel to the game-rich areas. It was thought America's supply of wild birds and beasts was inexhaustible, and there were no constraints, legal or otherwise, against killing them. The indiscriminate slaughter deprived future generations of much

Hunters slaughtered birds indiscriminately up to the time the Audubon Society's G.B. Grinnell initiated wildlife legislation.

of its wildlife heritage. In 1870 two herds of buffalo estimated at fifteen million animals roamed the land. By 1890 they were extinct.

Killing for pleasure: a trainload of hunters taking part in the extermination of the buffalo, which was accomplished with "the dispatch of a military campaign."

Spectator Sports

Big business — fraud — brutality

Baseball's reputation as a clean sport declined in the 1870's when gamblers rigged games.

During the 1870's and 1880's spectator sports provided the urban masses with some relief from the constriction of their surroundings, but, as usual, the cost was high. Boxing, baseball and horseracing became infested with criminal elements to the point where the terms "sporting man" and "gambler" became synonymous.

Horseracing, a sport that could not exist without wagers, fell into the hands of gambling syndicates. Race fixing was commonplace, and at Brighton Race Course in Brooklyn — "the swamp of the American turf" — the official timekeeper had "an eccentric watch."

Baseball had an even more disreputable name. A sports magazine of 1874 observed: "There is no sport now in vogue in which so much fraud prevails as in baseball. Any professional baseball club will throw a game if there is money . . . Horseracing is a pretty safe thing in comparison . . ."

It was not until after the formation of the National League in 1876 that the game began to free itself of gambling, bribery and the operation of illegal pools. Although heroes to the public, the many players who participated in these schemes had earlier been called by the *New York Times* "worthless, dissipated gladiators . . . not much above the professional pugilist."

Curiously, notwithstanding the *New York Times'* editorials against boxing, the fights of the period were unlikely to have been fixed, although they were invariably dirty. The early pugilists were brutal yet proud, the rules casual, and the contest did not end until one man had been at least punched, kicked and bitten into bloody unconsciousness. In July 1889 at Richburg, Miss., John L. Sullivan took 75 knockdown rounds in 106-degree heat to defeat Jake Kilrain; the fight lasted 2 hours, 16 minutes. The sport became so murderous that New York City outlawed it — which did nothing to diminish its popularity as the matches went "underground" to shady sections of Westchester and Staten Island or on rafts up the Hudson.

In all of these spectator sports, reform eventually had its way. Meanwhile they provided the Victorian public with a prism through which was accurately refracted the despair of their own lives.

Boxing degenerated into kicking matches that reached their apogee in the 75 rounds between Sullivan and Kilrain in 1889 — the last bare-knuckle fight.

Football

Violence as a leisure activity was
not a monopoly of the prize ring.
It was the only ingredient of college football, which seasonally
transformed intelligent young
men into grunting Neander-
thalers. Teams from the highest
institutes of learning fought
each other with a savagery worthy of the street gangs, leading to
widespread injuries and great
bitterness.

The Cornell University team,
particularly, was feared for its
aggressiveness, and in 1876 both
Harvard and Yale refused to meet
it. Not that Yale men were softies;
in 1884 they clashed with Princeton in a game that was described
in the *New York Evening Post:*
"The spectators could see the
eleven hurl themselves together
and build themselves into kicking, writhing heaps." Paul Bourget, the French novelist and critic,
attending another game, compared these melees with "an in-
extricable knot of serpents with
human heads . . . often after these
frenzied entanglements one of the
combatants remains on the field
motionless, so hard has he been
pressed, crushed and dumped."

At such barbaric contests, surgeons seemed just as important as
players. The casualty rate, often
seven players injured out of
twenty—nearly 33 percent—was
described wryly by F. L. Muirhead as greater than that of the
Battle of Bar Harbor, the bloodiest
clash of the Civil War.

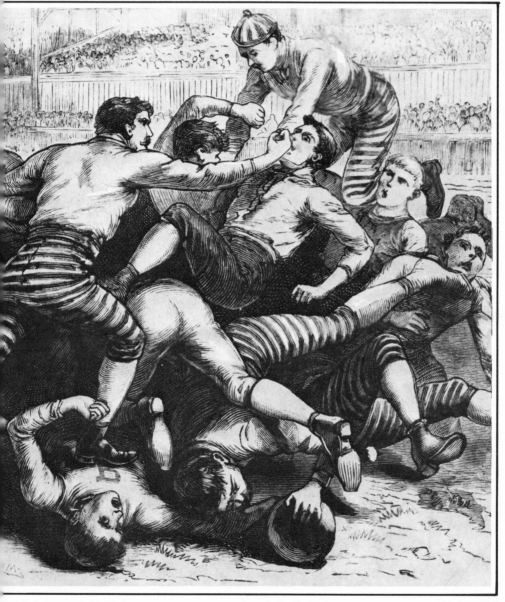

Good clean fun enjoyed by the aesthetic young men of Princeton and Yale.

Pastimes of the Young

"Their opportunities for mischief are greater than those for harmless amusement."

If recreational facilities for adults were limited, they were totally absent for children; in the scheme of things during the 1860's through the nineties, children simply did not count. City children, especially those from the slums, were virtual prisoners in hostile surroundings. Their playground was the street; their games, mischief and vandalism were born of utter boredom, a dull apathy that Jane Addams said "smothered the divine fire of youth." Some broke windows, others smashed street lamps, and in a few slum areas, according to Mayor Abram Hewitt of New York, young people amused themselves "in shooting policemen."

They fought continually; casual encounters led to quarrels, and before long the youngsters were "beating each other in the face,

Hatching mischief. Mulberry Bend, N.Y.—nothing to do, no place to go.

New York City docks—the park of the poor. Lacking fare to reach Central Park, tenement dwellers crowded along the waterfront. Children who took a swim were arrested.

rolling in the gutter like the little animals they are." City authorities provided no space, nor did they leave as much as a single vacant lot as a play area for the young. In 1895 the city of Boston donated three sand piles for the use of children—a radical step—and even by 1903 only eighteen cities had public playgrounds of any description.

Midcentury New York had some open lots where the young played stickball and football, but with new waves of immigrants these were appropriated for buildings, leading to the incongruity of more children and less playing area. Quite naturally, street games drew numerous complaints of annoyance and property damage from storekeepers, tenants and pedestrians. And whenever the police responded, they did so harshly. One macabre incident was recalled by Jacob Riis: "We have seen in New York a boy shot down by a policeman for the heinous crime of playing football in the street on Thanksgiving Day."

On election nights, it was an accepted tradition for city youngsters to build huge bonfires from wood they collected in their neighborhoods. In one incident an entire frame house was "carried away piecemeal and burned . . ." The police stood by dazed as the sky shone luridly all over town.

Summertime brought the young crowding to the dock areas in the hope of catching a cool breeze. But taking a swim was a "crime" for which those unlucky enough to be caught by the police were sent to prison.

Henry Bergh, the founder of the Society for the Prevention of Cruelty to Animals, once remarked that children needed to be taken out of bondage by an emancipation movement akin to that which liberated the slaves. . . .

Juvenile ebullience erupted on election nights, when gamins of New York stacked up ash barrels to make bonfires. Youngsters of other cities did likewise.

191

Fun with a gun

No doubt the framers of the Constitution did not intend it, but the gun became an integral part of America's household hardware and the all-time favorite toy of her children. Today there is widespread disapproval of firearms, but during the Victorian period even the most gentle families saw nothing immoral in allowing their children to play with guns—both real and the toy kind. In rural America it was almost a rite of puberty to give a boy his own gun, and marksmanship with a rifle and revolver was considered a highly desirable preparation for manhood.

The resulting culture gave the products of Remington, Colt and Winchester every bit the prestige of, and probably even greater popularity than, those of Walt Whitman or Mark Twain—especially among boys.

The mind
of the young
was poisoned,
it was felt,
by dime novels
that dwelled
on violence
and murder,
gangs and guns.

Toy pistols
were favorite
playthings,
ideal for training
future marksmen.

Babe in arms.

City Parks

Designed for repose and spiritual renewal, they were not immune to urban ills.

Leisure requires change, and protected green acreage offers vital relief to people overwhelmed by concrete. In the old days, however, such relief did not exist for masses of city residents.

In the 1870's in lower Manhattan—where most of the people lived—there was hardly a park worthy of the name. Central Park was far uptown, inaccessible to those for whom it would have been most beneficial. The "Central" referred to its location on Manhattan; in fact, it was four miles north of the population center in 1870, when the city had roughly 900,000 residents.

When Oliver Wendell Holmes visited the city he praised the park but complained that it had cost him four dollars to come uptown from 23rd Street and Fifth Avenue. Obviously the poor could not afford the horsecar fare; indeed it was said that "for the mass of people, the park might have been 100 miles away, too distant even for an annual outing." A teacher asking fifty slum children in 1873 how they liked Central Park learned to his surprise that only three had ever visited it.

The park's location reflected no discredit on its creator, Frederick Law Olmsted, and those lucky enough to have access to it were rewarded by its pleasant walks and tranquil beauty. However, even then, the fear of crime troubled both park commissioners and visitors. From the beginning, speculators who wanted the ground for building lots opposed the planned park on grounds that

With no parks to relax in, the poor sought refuge along New York's rugged riverfront.

it would become a hangout for gangsters and ruffians who "would rob decent citizens and drive them out by their bawdy antics." And they were not entirely wrong.

The park became a refuge for loafers, bums and thieves who, while not the most dangerous criminal types, made its visitors apprehensive. Olmsted expressed concern about these dangers in his 1870 report of the Parks Commission: "Difficulty of preventing ruffianism and disorder . . . was from the first the greatest the Commission met, and the means of overcoming it cost more study than all other things."

Bums and drunks were a constant annoyance, preempting benches that were "intended for

193

Park benches were favorite sleeping
quarters for derelicts and drunks.

Here in the golden summer hours,
Good nature thus abusing,
Sit lazy, idle good-for-naughts
Complacent in the snoozing.
The decent poor can find no place
Where all the tramps and bummers
Lie listless through the pleasant days
And spend the slothful summers.

the self-respecting toilers." Although the police made numerous arrests—as many as forty in one morning—the nuisance never disappeared, and park visitors wandered through its dales and tunnels with less than comfortable feelings. The sinister-looking denizens created a climate of fear that was responsible as much as crime itself for Olmsted's recommendation in 1882 that the park be closed after dark. Nothing came of it because of the impracticality of trying to lock up an 84-acre plot, despite the police warning that at night "there was an excellent chance of being garroted and robbed."

Further handicaps to pleasure were imposed by park officials themselves. Visitors were regimented rather ponderously, as if the park were a place to be viewed rather than used. Warnings to keep off the grass were strictly enforced; games and sports were frowned upon as they interfered with "the refined pleasure of landscape-watching."

Perhaps the best-known enclosed space in America, Central Park remains as it was in the good old days—alternately a focus of pleasure and apprehension but crucially an indispensable source of relaxation.

Central Park Lake was polluted by squatters, who used it as a dumping ground. Fear of malarial fever agitated the public in 1875.

Seaside Leisure

"Our beaches are defiled by accumulated junk"

A day's outing in the Gilded Age was seldom launched on impulse; instead it was plotted far in advance—like a minor campaign. For city residents—about two thirds of the population—getting out to the countryside or seashore was a considerable nuisance. It also entailed expenses that a working-class family could not readily afford. Even in the 1860's, when open country was close at hand, the *New York Journal* observed: "There is real moral heroism in the way some people attend picnics. They carry enormous baskets. They pack themselves into stages three deep, or wedge themselves into cars, or stand in the burning sun on the decks of steamboats." For New Yorkers the seashore provided the biggest lure—New Jersey's Long Beach attracting the well-to-do; Coney Island, the masses. Before the opening of the Bay Ridge streetcar line it took two and a half hours, by horsecar, ferry and boat, to travel from the city to Coney Island. The round trip cost $2 per person; a locker for changing (not permitted elsewhere) cost 50 cents, with queues two and three blocks long at peak season. But even more disagreeable than the time, the cost or the crowding was the condition of the beach itself. It was polluted. Polluted because New Yorkers used the waterways surrounding the city as dumping grounds for garbage, and much of this settled on the closer shoreline. The river dumping platforms were discontinued in 1872, but the new method of using dumping barges proved even more detrimental to beach cleanliness. In 1898 the erstwhile street-cleaning commissioner admitted that the city's garbage "defiled the beaches in an intolerable degree." Similarly, the Jersey shore was littered for miles with "boxes, cans, straw and other accumulated junk."

No doubt there were thousands of miles of pristine beach, but this was quite irrelevant to people who couldn't reach them. It was an irony typical of the period. Pollution overhead, garbage underfoot, streets choked with traffic, bursting slums, crime, labor unrest, dope addiction—problems of the future in the country with a future.

Perhaps the Victorians' obsession with success left little room for compassion. Perhaps their pursuit of happiness left little time for pleasure. Perhaps, indeed, our nostalgia more rightfully belonged to them as they cast a sad eye on the lowering sky and longed for the good old days.

Trains to Coney Island were overcrowded. It was an arduous trip to the not-so-clean beach.

Soft blow the lovely breezes
O'er Coney's sandy isle;
Where every prospect pleases,
And only man is vile.

Sources

Adamic, L., *Dynamite,* New York, 1934.
Adams, H. C., "Slaughter of Railroad Employees." *Forum* XIII (1892), p. 500.
Addams, J., *The Spirit of Youth and the City Streets,* New York, 1909.
Ade, G., *The Old Time Saloon,* New York, 1931.
Altgeld, P., *Our Penal Machinery and Its Victims,* Chicago, 1886.
Alwood, C. W., *Centennial History of Illinois,* Springfield, Ill., 1920.
American Railway, The, New York, 1889.
(A. P.) *Mysteries and Miseries of the Great Metropolis,* New York, 1874.
Asbury, H., *Sucker's Progress,* New York, 1938.
Ashby, I, "Child Labor in Southern Cotton Mills," *World's Work, II* (1901), p. 1290.
Astor, G., *The New York Cops,* New York, 1971.
Babcock, K. C., *The Scandinavian Element,* Urbana, Ill., 1941.
Bartlett, G. B., "Recreation of People," *Journal of Social Science,* XII (1880), p. 141.
Beard, C. and M., *Basic History of the United States,* New York, 1960.
Beecher, C., *Principles of Domestic Science,* New York, 1870.
Bell, D., *The End of Ideology,* Glencoe, Ill., 1960, p. 137.
Bennett, A., *Your United States,* New York, 1912.
Bernstein, N. J., *Towards a New Past,* New York, 1968.
Bimba, A., *The History of the American Working Class,* New York, 1927.
Blanke, E. N., "Cliffdwellers," *Review of Reviews,* Vol. VIII (1893), p. 205.
Bolce, H., "Horse versus Health," *Appleton's Journal,* Vol. II (1908), p. 532.
Bourget, C. J. P., *Outre Mer,* New York, 1895.
Brace, C. L., *The Dangerous Classes of New York,* 1872.
Brecher, J., *Strike,* San Francisco, 1972.
Bremner, R., *Children and Youth in America,* Vol. II, Parts 1 and 2, 1866–1932, Cambridge, Mass., 1971.
———, *From the Depths,* New York, 1956.
Brieger, G. H., *Medical America in the 19th Century,* Baltimore, Md., 1972.
Brooks, J. C., *As Others See Us,* New York, 1908.
———, *The Social Unrest,* New York, 1903.
Brown, D., *The Gentle Tamers,* New York, 1958.
Brown, E. L., *Physician and Medical Care in the Perspective of a Century,* New York, 1937.
Brown, H. C., *New York in the Elegant Eighties,* New York, 1926.
Browne, J. H., *The Great Metropolis,* Hartford, Conn., 1869.
———, *The Problem of Living in New York,* H.M. Vol. 65 (1882), p. 918.
Bruce, R., *1877, Year of Violence,* Indianapolis, 1959.
Brydges, *Uncle Sam at Home,* New York, 1888.
Buel, J. W., *City Life Unveiled,* Philadelphia, 1882.
Burne-Jones, P., *Dollars and Democracy,* New York, 1904.
Burnham, A., "Apartment Houses," *Dictionary of American History,* Supp. I, 1961, p. 16.
Calhoun, H. T., *The Social History of the American Family,* Vol. III, New York, 1945.
Calkins, A., *The Opium Habit,* Philadelphia, 1871.
Campbell, H., *Darkness and Daylight,* Hartford, Conn., 1891.
———, *Prisoners of Poverty,* Boston, 1881.
Capers, G., "Yellow Fever in Memphis," in Kramer and Holborn, *The City in American Life,* New York, 1970, p. 172.
Chapin, H. D., "Crowded Schools as Promoters of Disease," *Forum,* Vol. XIX (1895), p. 296.
Chase, M. E., *A Goodly Heritage,* New York, 1932.
Chase, S., "Two Cheers for Technology," *Saturday Review,* February 20, 1971, p. 19.
Cleghorn, S. N., *Poems of Peace and Freedom,* New York, 1945.
Clews, H., "The Folly of Organized Labor," *North American Review,* Vol. 142 (1886), p. 601.
Cole, A. C., *The Irrepressible Conflict,* New York, 1934.
Commons, H. D., *History of Labor,* New York, 1918–1935.
Comstock, A., *Traps for the Young,* New York, 1890.
Cooper, P., *The Bellevue Story,* New York, 1948.
Council of Hygiene and Public Health Citizens' Association, *A Report,* New York, n.d.
Crafts, F. W., *What the Temperance Century Made Certain,* New York, 1885.

Cranshaw, L. A., *The Transformation of the School,* New York, 1961.

Crapsey, E., *The Nether Side of New York,* New York, 1872.

Crosby, E. H., "The Saloon as a Political Power," *Forum,* VII (1889), p. 323.

Crow, C., *The Great American Customer,* New York, 1943.

Cummings, R. O., *The American and His Food,* Chicago, 1940.

Curtis, W. B., "The Increase of Gambling and its Forms," *Forum,* XII (1891), p. 281.

Cutler, J. B., *Lynch Law,* New York, 1905.

Darrow, C., *Farmington,* New York, 1904.

Davis, B. A., "The Curse of Education," *North American Review,* Vol. 168 (1899), p. 164.

Day, H. B., *The Opium Habit,* Philadelphia, 1871.

Deutsch, A., *The Mentally Ill in America,* New York, 1949.

Department of Street Cleaning, *A Report,* New York, 1886.

Dexter, E. G., *The History of Education in the U.S.,* New York, 1904.

Dibble, F. L., *Vagaries of Sanitary Science,* Philadelphia, 1893.

Dick, E., *The Sod-House Frontier,* New York, 1937.

Dorsey, E. B. *English and American Railroads Compared,* New York, 1887.

Du Bois, W. E. B. "A Negro Schoolmaster in the New South," *Atlantic Monthly,* Vol. 83 (1889), p. 100.

Duffus, R. L., *Nostalgia: or If You Don't Like the 1960's Why Don't You Go Back Where You Came From?* New York, 1969.

Dulles, F. R., *America Learns to Play,* New York, 1940.

———, *Labor in America,* New York, 1940.

Dunlap, R., *Doctors of the American Frontier,* New York, 1965.

Durant, J., *Yesterday in Sports, New York,* 1956.

Eaton, D. B., "Despotism in Insane Asylums," *North American Review,* Vol. 132 (1881), p. 263.

Eggleston, E., *The Hoosier Schoolmaster,* 1871.

Eggleston, N. H., *Villages and Village Life,* New York, 1878.

Elbridge, B. P., and W. B. Watts, *Our Rival the Rascal,* Boston, 1897.

Ellsbree, W. S., *The American Teacher,* New York, 1939.

Elwood, C. A., "Has Crime Increased Since 1880?" *Journal of the American Institute of Criminal Law,* Vol. I (1910), p. 376.

Faithful, E., *Three Visits to America,* New York, 1884.

Felt, J. P., *Hostages of Fortune: Child Labor Reform in New York State,* Syracuse, New York, 1965.

Fife, E. D., *Social and Industrial Conditions during the Civil War,* New York, 1910.

Flagg, E., *The New York Tenement House Evil,* New York, 1895.

Fletcher, H. J. "Doom of the Small Town," *Forum,* XIX (1895), pp. 214 ff.

Flynt, J., *The World of Graft,* New York, 1901.

Furnas, J. C., *The Americans,* New York, 1969.

Garland, H., *Son of the Middle Border,* New York, 1925.

———, "Under the Lion's Paw," in *Main Travelled Roads,* Cambridge, Mass., 1891.

Gilson, M. B., *What's Past is Prologue,* New York, 1923.

Ginger, R., *Altgelt's America,* New York, 1962.

Ginzberg, E., and H. Berman, *The American Worker in the 20th Century,* New York, 1969.

Gladden, W., "The Embattled Farmer," *Forum,* X (1890), p. 315.

Glazier, W., *Peculiarities of American Cities,* Philadelphia, 1893.

Hamilton, G., *The Common School System,* Boston, 1890.

Handlin, O., *This Was America,* Cambridge, Mass., 1949.

Hendrick, B. J., "Street Railroad Financiers," *McClure's,* XXX, 1908, 337.

Hertzler, A. E., *The Horse and Buggy Doctor,* New York, 1938.

Hobson, C., *Recollections of a Happy Life,* New York, 1916.

Hogenboom, A. and O., *The Gilded Age,* Englewood Cliffs, N.J., 1967.

Holmes, O. W., *Medical Essays,* Boston, 1891.

Hopp, E. A., "Pen Sketches of American Life," in Handlin, *op. cit.,* p. 327.

Howe and Hummel, *Danger!* Buffalo, 1886.

Howells, W. D., *Impressions and Experiences,* New York, 1896.

———, *Suburban Sketches,* New York, 1871.

Hunter, R., *Poverty,* New York, Torchbook edition, 1965.

Huxley, A., "The History of Tension," *Annals of the New York Academy of Sciences,* Vol. 67 (1957), p. 678.

Johnson, A., *Pioneer's Progress,* New York, 1952

Johnson, R. U., *Remembered Yesterdays*, Boston, 1923.
Katz, M. B., *The Irony of Early School Reform in Mid-Century Massachusetts*, Cambridge, Mass., 1965.
Keller, M., "Alcohol in Health and Disease" *Annals, New York Academy of Sciences*, Vol. 133 (1966), p. 820.
Kennedy, M. F., *Schoolmaster of Yesterday*, New York, 1940.
Kingsbury, F. F., "The Tendency of Men to Live in Cities," *Journal of Social Science*, XXXIII (1895).
Kipling, R., *American Notes*, Philadelphia, 1885.
Knight, E. N., *The Influence of Reconstruction on Education in the South*, New York, 1913.
Lesy, M., *Wisconsin Death Trip*, New York, 1973.
Lexow Committee: *Report of the State Committee to Investigate the Police Department of New York*, Albany, 1885.
Lindsey, B. B., *The Dangerous Life*, New York, 1931.
Lombroso, C., "Why Homicide Has Increased in the United States," *North American Review*, Vol. 156 (1897), pp. 641 f.
Lynes, R., *The Domesticated Americans*, New York, 1957.
Lyon, P., *To Hell in a Daycoach*, Philadelphia, 1967.
Maddox, J. R., *The Doomsday Syndrome*, New York, 1972.
Maltbie, M. E., "A Century of Franchise History," *Municipal Affairs*, Vol. V (1902), p. 201.
Mandelbaum, S. J., *Boss Tweed's New York*, New York, 1965.
McCabe, J. D., *New York by Sunlight and Gaslight*, Philadelphia, 1882.
———, *Lights and Shadows of New York Life*, Philadelphia, 1872.
McClure, S. S., "The Increase of Lawlessness in the United States," *McClure's*, Vol. XXIV (1904), p. 168.
McKelvey, B., *History of American Prisons*, Chicago, 1936.
Maxwell, W. H., *A Quarter Century of School Development*, New York, 1912.
Mayer, G. M., *Once Upon a City*, New York, 1955.
Meltzer, M., *Bread and Roses, American Labor, 1865–1915*, New York, 1967.
Moore, E. C., *Fifty Years of American Education*, Boston, 1919.
Morris, L., *Incredible New York*, New York, 1951.
———, *Oscar Wilde in America*, New York, 1956.
Mower, S., *Memoirs of a Hotelman*, Boston, 1912.
Muirhead, J. F., *The Land of Contrasts*, New York, 1898.
Mumford, L., *The Brown Decade*, New York, Dover edition, 1955.
———, *The City in History*, New York, 1961.
———, *The Highway and the City*, New York, 1955.
Musto, D. F., *The American Disease*, New Haven, Conn., 1873.
Nelson, H. L., "Degraded Labor in Coalmines," *Harper's Weekly*, 1888, June 16.
Nevins, A., *Abram Hewitt*, New York, 1935.
———, *The Emergence of Modern America*, New York, 1937.
New York State Board of Health, *4th Report*, Albany, 1881.
Nichols, F. H., "Children of the Coal Shadow," *McClure's*, XX (1903), p. 435.
Nichols, T. L., "Work and Play in America," *Annals of American History*, Vol. 9, Chicago, 1967, p. 540.
Olmsted, F. L., "Public Parks and Enlargement of Towns," *Journal of Social Science*, 1871, p. 5.
———, "Spoils of the Park," in A. Fine, *Landscape and City Scape*, Ithaca, New York, 1967.
Parkhurst, C., *My Fifty Years in New York*, New York, 1923.
Peabody, F. G. "The Liquor Problem," Committee of Fifty, Boston, 1903.
Penniman, J. H. "Criminal Crowding of Public Schools," *Forum*, XIX (1896), p. 289.
Pickhard, M. E., and R. C. Burley, *The Midwest Pioneer*, New York, 1946.
Pierce, B. L., *As Others See Chicago*, Chicago, 1933.
Pilat, O., and J. Ransom, *Sodom on the Sea*, New York, 1941.
Plumb, J. B., *The Death of the Past*, New York, 1968.
Plunkett, H. M., *Women, Plumbers and Doctors*, New York, 1885.
Purdy, C., "Why We Get Sick," *North American Review*, 1897.
Pusey, W. A., *A Doctor of the 1870's and 1880's*, Springfield, Ill., 1935.
Rattray, J., *Dangers of New York Harbor*, New York, 1973.
Ravenal, M. P., *A Century of Public Health*, New York, 1921.
Reed, H. H., *Central Park: A History and a Guide*, New York, 1967.

Reeves, A. B., "Our Industrial Juggernaut," *Everybody's Magazine*, XVI, February, 1907.

Rice, J. R., *The Public School System in the U.S.*, New York, 1893.

Richardson, J., *The New York Police*, New York, 1970.

Richardson, J. H., "New Homes in New York," *Scribner's*, Vol. III (1874), p. 63.

Riis, J., *Battle with the Slums*, New York, 1902.

———, "The Children of the Poor," in R. A. Woods, *The Poor in Great Cities*, New York, 1895.

———, *How the Other Half Lives*, New York (Dover Edition), 1890.

Rischkin, M., *The Promised City*, New York, 1959.

Rosen, G., *A History of Public Health*, New York, 1958.

Rosenberg, C., *The Cholera Years*, Chicago, 1962.

Rothman, D., *The Discovery of the Asylum*, Boston, 1971.

Schlesinger, A. M., *The Rise of the City*, New York, 1933.

———, *Paths to the Present*, New York, 1949, "Food in the Making of America."

Schnapper, A. M., *American Labor*, Washington, D.C., 1972.

Shaler, N. S., *The United States of America*, New York, 2 vols., 1894.

Shaw, M. A., "The Public School System in a Boss-ridden City," *World's Work*, VII (1903–1904), p. 4204.

Shryock, R., *Medicine in America*, Baltimore, 1966.

Smalley, E. V., "The Isolation of Life on Prairie Farms," *Atlantic Monthly*, LXXXII, (1893), p. 379.

Smith, M. H., *Sunshine and Shadow in New York*, Hartford, Conn., 1869.

Smith, P., *Daughters of the Promised Land*, Boston, 1970.

Smith, S., *The City That Was*, New York, 1911.

Spahr, C. B., *America's Working People*, New York, 1900.

Spargo, R., *The Bitter Cry of Children*, New York, 1906.

Spencer, H., "Interview with Dr. Youmans," in A. Nevins, *America Through British Eyes*, New York, 1948.

Stern, B. J., *American Medical Practice*, New York, 1945.

Stevenson, R. A., "The Poor in Summer," *Scribner's*, XXXX (1901), p. 264.

Stevenson, R. L., *Across the Plains*, New York, 1892.

———, "Steerage Scenes," in J. D. Hart, ed., *From Scotland to Silverado*, Cambridge, Mass., 1966.

Stewart, D., "Unsanitary Schools and Public Indifference," *Forum*, XX (1903), p. 103.

Streighthoff, F. H., *The Standard of Living Among Industrial People of America*, Boston, 1911.

Strong, G. T., *Diaries*, eds. A. Nevins and M. H. Thomas, 4 vols., New York, 1952.

Tarr, J., "Urban Pollution . . . many long years ago," *American Heritage*, Vol. XXIII (1971), p. 65.

Thernstrom, S., "Urbanization, Migration and Social Mobility," in B. J. Bernstein, op. cit.

Thomson, C., "Waste by Fire," *Forum*, II (1886), p. 27.

Twain, M., *Mark Twain's Travels with Mr. Brown*; eds. F. Walker and E. Dane, New York, 1940.

Tyack, G., *Turning Points in American Education*, Waltham, Mass. 1967.

Tyler, A. F., *Freedom's Ferment*, Minneapolis, 1944.

Van Vorst, J. M., *The Cry of Children*, New York, 1908.

Voight, D. Q., *American Baseball*, Norman, Oklahoma, 1966.

Walker, J. B., *Fifty Years of Rapid Transit, 1864–1917*, New York, 1918.

Walling, G. W., *Recollections of a New York Police Chief*, New York, 1898.

Waring, G. E., *Street Cleaning*, New York, 1897.

Warren, J. H., *Thirty Years' Battle with Crime or "The Crying Shame of Cities,"* Poughkeepsie, N.Y., 1875.

Wells, H. G., *The Future of America*, New York, 1906.

Werner, M. R., *Tammany Hall*, New York, 1932.

Wheatley, W. W., "Transporting New York's Millions," *World's Work*, Vol. VI (1903), p. 3422.

Wiley, H. W., *Foods and their Adulteration*, New York, 1907.

———, *An Autobiography*, New York, 1930.

Windmiller, L., "Vexations of a City Pedestrian," *Municipal Affairs*, Vol. VI (1902), p. 130.

Wingate, C. F., "The Unsanitary Homes of the Rich," *North American Review*, Vol. 137 (1883), p. 172.

Wood's Illustrated Handbook of New York, New York, 1872.

Notes

Key to Abbreviations

A.A.H.	Annals of American History
A.M.	Atlantic Monthly
C.M.	Century Magazine
D.A.H.	Dictionary of American History
H.H.	Hearth and Home
H.M.	Harper's Magazine
H.W.	Harper's Weekly
J.S.S.	Journal of Social Science
M.A.	Municipal Affairs
Mc.C.	McClure's Magazine
L.I.N.	Leslie's Illustrated Newspaper
N.A.R.	North American Review
N.Y.D.G.	New York Daily Graphic
N.Y.T.	New York Times
W.W.	World's Work

1 AIR

1 Smoke and prosperity: Gilson, 8. Smoke as a cure: Glazier, 334. Cesspools: Schlesinger, Rise, 102.

2 Pigs in city streets: Cole. 179; Alwood III/4.5. Equine pollution: Tarr, Bolce.

4.5 Hunter's Point inquiry: N.Y. State Board, 4; H.W. 1881, August 20; ibid. 1884, February 23.

7-9 Street odor: Strong II/178. Ashbarrels, garbage: Brydges, 103; Waring, 9; Mandelbaum, 165. Discarded vehicles: Department 1886, 51. Harbor obstruction: H.W. 1884, Sept. 27.

10 Wherever wind blows: N.Y.D.G. 1887, June 10. Summer: Zeitloff, 554; Riis, Other Half, 56.

12 "Great foul city . . ." Campbell, Prisoners, 245.

14 Chicago, early drainage: Ginger, 23, 24. Air: "Having seen it": Kipling, 334; Pierce, 278.

16.17 Pittsburgh: "Noisome vomit": Handlin, 407, 409. Laundry bills: Mumford, City, 474 "They don't notice smoke": Glazier, 334. Frontier towns: Dick, 394. "Sidewalks, swimming, rafts": L.I.N. 1879, 249.

2 TRAFFIC

19 New York: Center of population: Mandelbaum, 12. "Cats late for appointment": Burne-Jones, 21.

20-24 Ruffians in streetcars: Browne, Metrop. 471. Foul air: McCabe, 187; Strong, II 97. Crowding: Howells, Suburban, 110; Nevins, Hewitt, 496.

22-23 Crossing Broadway: Warren, 362. H.H., 1872, Dec. 14. Street safety: Newsweek, 1972, March 16. "Tearing up Broadway": H.W. 1891, Sept. 26. "Vast chasms": Burne-Jones, 80. "Encumbrances": M.A. VI (1903) 130.

24-25 Railcrossing in towns: McClure, Faithful, 155. Mumford, City, 461.

27 New York made for railroads: Browne, Metropolis, 23.

28 Speculators: N.Y.D.G. 1879, July 16. "End of urban acceptability": Mumford, Highway, 240.

29 Winter: Waring, 15; H.W. 1887, Jan 22.

30 Tram car speed: W.W. 1902, 3425; Hendrick, 337. New anxiety: N.Y. Daily Tribune, 1890, Sept. 18. Quoted: Mayer, 295.

31 "Cry for discipline": Wells, 58.

General Literature: Maltbie; Walker; Windmiller.

3 HOUSING

32.33 "Lady with diamonds": Muirhead, 193, Schlesinger, Rise, 83. Living expenses: McCabe, N.Y. 62–63.

34.35 Constantly demanding structures: Lynes, 156. Sooty air: Wingate.

36 "I am the Landlord": N.Y.D.G. 1882, Feb. 6. High rents: Browne, Problem. Mark Twain, 109.

37 Boarding House: Lynes, 39 ff.

38 Apartment Houses: Burnham; Blanke. Deterioration: M.M. Vol. 6, p. 341.

39 Fires: Thomson; Schlesinger, Rise, 105; Mumford, Brown Decade, 138.

40.41 Defamation of word "home": Streightoff, 77. Strong IV, 96. "They were only foreigners": Gilson 8. Squatters: H.M. 61 (1880) p. 568.

42.43 Rents in slum districts: McCabe, Light, 406. "Astonishing feature": Handlin, 411. Schlesinger, Rise, 111; S. Smith, 88.

44.45 Depravity: Brace, 223; Felt, 4. Streetboys: M.H. Smith, 367; Brace, 110; Strong II/57. Case of Mary Ellen: Bremner, Children II/i, 186.

4 COUNTRY

51 55 Poisoned Wells: N. H. Eggleston, 164. "I knew a doctor": Dufus, 37.

52 Flies: Dick, 237. Window screens: Lynes, 129.

53 Heating, air: Shaler II, 574; Beecher, 40; Plunkett, 49.

54.55 Tramp evil: Nevins, Emergence, 301. The Nation, 1878, Jan. 24.

56.57 Children on the farm: Kennedy, 234. "Waste filled yard": N. H. Eggleston, 17. "A great deal of land but little country": Brydges, 151.

58 Mortgages: Beard, 373. Populist Revolt: Hogenboom, 176.

60 Insect plagues: Dick, 202. Prairie fires: D.A.H. II/276.

62.63 Loneliness: Smalley; Babcock, 136–137; Schlesinger, Rise, 58.

64.65 Lure of City: Kingsbury; Thernstrom. "If I were offered deed": Olmsted, Public, 5. Schlesinger, Rise, 60. Cremin, 75.

5 LABOR

67 "Never have the rich . . .": Meltzer, 53, 54.

68 Laboring man: Clews. Hours in steelmills: Commons III, 99. Tempo of work: Brooks, Unrest, 186. Old age: Spahr, 155.

70-71 Accidents: Reeves; Adams; Hunter, 37. Bruce, 31. Handlin, 408. Funeral expenses: Bremner, Children, II/1, 637.

72-74 Sweatshops: No time to eat: Spargo, 37; Campbell, Prisoners, 133. Female slaves of N.Y.: L.I.N. 1888, Nov. 3, p. 191.

75 A. T. Stewart girls: M. H. Smith, 59; Ginzberg: 101

76-78 Child labor: "We take them . . ." Calhoun III/137. Work: good for children: Spahr, 8. Cold water dashed in face: Ashby. Fall asleep with full mouth: Ginzberg, 129. ". . . shipped like hogs.": Van Vorst, Cry, XIX. The golf links: Cleghorn.

80.81 Living expenses: Hunter, 117; Spahr 153. Unemployment: Ginzberg, 32; Bimba, 157.

82 "We struck . . .": Manifesto of Pullman strikers. Strikes heighten police power: Adamic, 36. How to treat rioters: Independent 1877, Aug. 2.

84 Machine creates jobs: Brooks, Unrest, 180. Life of Victorian worker: Maddox, 180.

General Literature: Dulles; Felt; Ginzberg; Schnapper.

6 CRIME

87 Increase in Crime: Bell; Elwood; Lombroso; McClure.

88.89 03 Crime: Gramercy Park: Strong IV/241; Wood, p. 27. Wilds of Africa: L.I.N. 1867, Sept. 21. Dance Hall visit: Browne, Metrop. 278. "History of American cities . . .". D.A.H. III/252.

90 Juvenile Delinquents: "no occupation": H.W. 1869, Feb. 6. Brace, 27; Ravenal, 295. Prisons: Lindsey, 49; Altgeld, 31.

92-97 "Last prop . . . cop": N.Y.D.G. 1879, June 18. Municipal versus Metropolitan: Walling, 60. Telegraph: Richardson, 170. Prisoners beaten: Lexow IV/3598; Mandelbaum, 52; Richardson, 190. Statistics juggled: McCabe, Sunlight, 351. Police graft: Stipend larger than salaries. Warren, 77, 148; Browne, Metrop. 57.

98 Prostitution, licentiousness: Parkhurst Sermon, 1892, March 13. "Sex a commodity": E. Blackwell, quoted in Smith, 228. "Prostitutes solicit . . .": Morris, New York, 31.

100.101 "Greedy men stealing . . .": Werner, XIII. American acquiescence: Spencer, 353. "Don't want city scrubbed out": Flynt, 56. Politicking more profitable than stealing. McCabe, p. 544. Elections: Astor, 56. Auditor of public accounts: Crapsy, 10.

102 "No one respects . . .": Chicago Daily News, 1903. Lawcourts: Walling, 572 ff.

104 Prisons: Schlesinger, Rise, 360. "Tombs more Egyptian than Christian": Crafts, 114. Great walled cages: McKelvey, 146.

106 Lynching: Atrocities . . . Nation, 69 (1899), p. 440; Cutler.

General Literature: Astor; Crapsy; Elbridge; Mandelbaum; Warren.

7 FOOD

110.111 Emaciated cattle: Cummings, 96. Unwholesome meat: Dibble, 221. Bob veal traffic: F.L.I.N. 1887, April 16. Food deterioration: Report, 59.

114 Swill Milk Scandal: H.W. 1870, Jan. 22.

116 "Butter an enormity": Beecher, 148, 157. Bogus butter scandal: L.I.N. 1884, March 29.

118 Adulteration: Warren, 267 ff; Wiley.

120 Children's food: Spargo 90 ff; Browne, Metropolis, 274 ff.

122 "Gobble, gulp, go": Schlesinger, Food, 241. Hasty cooking: Faithful, 54; Beecher, 138. Hasty meals: Handlin, 414. Clatter of plates . . .: Browne, Metropolis, 262. Boarding House food: Lynes, 40.

126 Western food: Shaler, II, 574.

129 Increase in drinking: Schlesinger, Rise, 360. Whiskey rectifiers: Wiley, Food, 204. "Liquor important as printer's ink": Tyler, 311. Girl drunkard: Astor, 30. Converting . . . rye to rum: Crow, 129. "Whole families died drunkards": Greeley quote in American Heritage Cook Book, N.Y., 1964, p. 91. "Drunkenness causes misery": T. V. Powderly. Drink and crime: Encycl. Soc. Science, I, 626.

General Literature: Food: Cummings; Wiley; Young. Drink: Ade; Keller; Peabody.

8 HEALTH

135 Technology and medicine: Shryock, 71.

136.137 Yellow fever in the South: Capers.

138.139 Sanitation: Walling, 166. Dr. Bigg rebuked: D.A.H. Vol. V, p. 328.

General Literature: Ravenal; Rosen; Rosenberg; Smith.

140 "He ain't sick": Pickard and Burley, 16. Illness on frontier: Dick, 434.

142.143 "Git up every night . . .": Hertzler, 39. Harvard students cannot write: Nevins,

277. Doctors "pure tradesmen": Shryock, 60. Drugging: Stern, 19. "Materia medica": Holmes, 203.

144 Attire of country surgeon: Hertzler, 6. Knife-happy surgeons: Brieger, 203. Garfield died of infection: Brieger, 201.

146 "Nurse slept in bath tub": Hobson, 81. Bellevue Hospital: Cooper. Rats in hospital: Brieger, 234. Crowded as tenement: Mayer, 341.

148-151 Alienist not a jailer: Brieger, 223. Cruelty: Eaton. Idleness: The Nation, 1876, p. 199. Increase of Insanity: Brydges, p. 71.

152 "Apocalypse of Horror": Hogenboom, 139. William James experiments: Huxley. Doctors use morphine: Pusey, 96. Youth and drugs: Addams, 55.

General Literature: Deutsch; Musto; Ravenal; Rosen; Rosenberg; Rothman.

9 EDUCATION

155 "Expect to learn nothing": Johnson, 40.

156 Yankee demagoguery: Cole, 206. Teacher boarding around: Tyack, 414. "Seldom had same teacher": Darrow, 52.

157 "Lickin' and larnin'": E. Eggleston, 53. "Trees in yard": D. Brown, 287. Baseness of boys: Kennedy, 144.

158 Unruliness: Tyack, 268. Visiting boys attacked: Johnson, 43.

160 Negro education: Tyack, 268; Dexter, 265; Knight, 78 ff; DuBois.

162 Schools: refuse vault: N.Y.D.G., 1889, February 18. Factory of hunchbacks: Chapin. Criminal crowding: Penniman. Air quality: Riis, Playgrounds. Teacher gives baths: Cranshaw, 71. Noise: Stewart.

166-168 Teaching methods: Rice. Children not to talk: Darrow, 171. Hungry children: Spargo, 117. Teachers subsist on pittance: N.Y.T., 1879, March 9; Ellsbree, 431. Favoritism: N.Y.T., 1877, March 15. Boss dominance: Shaw.

169 Grading overwork: Davis; H.W., 1892, Nov. 11; Maxwell, 135.

General Literature: Hamilton; Katz, Knight.

10-11 TRAVEL AND LEISURE

171 Railway accidents: Brooks, Unrest, 210.

172-174 Horrors of Emigrant Ships: H.W., 1869, 206. "A dim inferno": Stevenson, Steerage, 22. Noah's Ark, lack of civility: Stevenson, Across, 6.

176 Desolate Stations: Brydges, 151. Grime and smoke: Amer. Railway, 234. Discomfort: Railroad Gaz., Vol. 17 (1885), 300. Passengers unhappy: M. Twain, 123. Schedules: Duffus, 27; Mower, 118.

177 "Infernal dormitories": Handlin, 301. "Malodorous promiscuity": Bennett, 103. Station meals: Morris, Wilde, 232.

178 Commuting: Wheatley. "Suburbanly bundled men": Howells, 86.

180.181 Ferry dangers: McCabe, Lights, 303. Disasters: Rattray. Slocum Disaster: Munsey's Mag. Vol. 33 (1904), p. 321. Western Steamers: Dunlap, 88.

183 No leisure: Nichols, T. L.

184 Gambling and lust for work: Handlin, 327; Warren, 280; Curtis; Asbury.

187 Baseball: Voight, 82. Horse racing: Mayer, 294.

188 Football: Bourget, 326. Casualty rate: Muirhead, 116.

190 Opportunity for mischief: Riis, Children, 86. Shooting policemen: Nevins, Hewitt, 505. Boy shot down: Riis, Battle, 223

208 Holmes visits park: Reed, 34. Park unknown to slum children: P. A. Stevenson, For the poor . . . miles away: Olmsted, Public Parks, 30. Chance of being garrotted: Olmsted, Spoils, 413.

196 Polluted beaches: H.W. 1898, July 9. Coney Island: Pilat and Ransom.

Acknowledgments

I consider myself fortunate to have had as my editor Robert Loomis, who caught my idea on the wing and guided me with infinite skill and patience from first word to last.

In the preparation of the text I have had the assistance of Terence Flanagan, whose skills as a writer and editor have brought my theme into sharper focus.

Miss Gilda Roberts acted as my editorial assistant and handled research assignments expertly and with untiring alacrity.

For contributing to our picture coverage, for guidance and suggestions, I would like to express my thanks to the following individuals:

Lionel A. Atwill
John S. Blay
Allan Burnham
John Caldwell
Adrienne Coleman
Dr. Robert Cranco
Anita Duncan
Audrie Furcon
William Gallagher
Suzanne H. Gallup
Frank Jay
Mark Keller

R. J. Peszek
Henry Hope Reed
Mrs. Paul M. Rhyner
Charles C. Roundy
Helen Ruskell
M. B. Schnapper
Lea Smits
Robert P. Smith
Dorothy Swanson
Ellen Stolzman
Alice Weaver
James Wilson

Many libraries, government agencies and science centers have helped me in my research, pictorial and textual:

Bancroft Library
Carnegie Library
Library of Congress
Montana Historical Society
Museum of the City of New York
National Institute of Alcohol Abuse
National Safety Council

New York Public Library
New York Society Library
New Canaan Library
Rutgers Center of Alcoholic
  Studies
Steamship Historical Society
Tamamint Institute

About the Author

OTTO L. BETTMANN is the founder of the famed Bettmann Archive in New York, one of the world's great picture libraries. Its resources, some three million prints and photographs, are used all over the world by publishers, educators, ad men and the audio-visual media.

Expelled during the Nazi regime from his post as Curator of Rare Books at the Prussian State Art Library in Berlin, Dr. Bettmann came to America in 1935 where he established the Archive and became widely known as a graphic historian.

Among his previous publications are *As We Were: Family Life in America, A Pictorial History of Medicine, Our Literary Heritage* (with Van Wyck Brooks) and *The Bettmann Portable Archive.*

He lives with his wife, an interior designer, in Pound Ridge, New York. During the winter months, Dr. Bettmann directs a new Department of Pictorial Research at the Learning Resources Center of Florida Atlantic University of Boca Raton.